MECHANISM
OF SUCCESS:

ATTRACTING the Life Your Want

Other books by Kolie Crutcher

Electric Living: The Science behind the Law of Attraction

MECHANISM OF SUCCESS

ATTRACTING THE LIFE YOU WANT

KOLIE CRUTCHER

BETTIE YOUNGS BOOKS

About the Cover:
The inspiration behind this book's cover is to bring into plain view the invisible mechanism that is attracting the circumstances of your life. The vertical spiral is the wire (arranged in coils) of the electromagnet. The lines emanating from the center and from the ends of the spiral are the normally invisible force lines of the electromagnetic field, which are produced as electric current flows through the wire. These electromagnetic force lines cannot be seen, smelled, heard, touched, or tasted by the senses. Yet these invisible electromagnetic force lines attract visible pieces of iron and steel. The aim of this book—as inspired by the cover—is to bring into the reader's conscious view the invisible force that results from his Thinking. In both the electromagnet and mankind, there is an unseen calculated process—an attractive mechanism—at work. Unless we learn to "see" the attractive force of the mechanism, success will be difficult, if not impossible to attain.

Cover Design by Luis Llanos
Text Design by Jane Hagaman
Author Photo by Ron Warner

Bettie Youngs Book Publishers
www.BettieYoungsBooks.com

If you are unable to order this book from your local bookseller, or from wholesalers Baker & Taylor or Ingram, or online from Amazon or Barnes & Noble, or from Espresso, or Read How You Want (Large Print, Braille, Daisy), you may order directly from the publisher: sales@BettieYoungsBooks.com

ISBN: 978-1-940784-59-5
eBook: 978-1-940784-60-1
Audio available online from Audible.com.

Library of Congress Control Number available upon request.
1. Kolie Crutcher. 2. Law of Attraction. 3. Self-Expression. 4. Rubik Cube. 5. Consciousness. 6. Metaphysics. 7. Sense of Self. 8. Goals. 9. Relationships. 10. Success. 11. Mind Science. 12. Self-Discipline. 13. Achievement. 14. Electromagnetism. 15. Mind Set. 16. Thinking. 17. Mechanism of Success. 18. Power of Focus. 19. Higher Power.

This book is dedicated to:

VY & JKM

Acknowledgments

I am eternally grateful to God for inner strength, light and love.

My deep appreciation goes to Bettie Youngs of Bettie Youngs Book Publishing Co. for her diligent professionalism and sincere efforts in making this book happen. Her guidance and belief in me is an invaluable asset. Her company published my previous book, *Electric Living: The Science behind the Law of Attraction*, a book that is now published in a good number of languages throughout the world; I am most pleased and honored to have such a stellar world-wide reader base.

I want to express my greatest appreciation to my mother, father, sisters and grandparents. This work would not be possible without their unconditional love, support, respect and guidance.

And finally, I appreciate you—the reader—for choosing to read this book. Let us always be connected through these pages.

Table of Contents

A Message from the Author

This book is short. The brevity is intentional, and for several reasons. First, *the mechanism of success is simple*. Notice I didn't say *easy*, but rather, *simple*.

Secondly, I have previously written a book (*Electric Living: The Science behind the Law of Attraction*) that *details* the science behind the law of success at work. Those principles are still the same. This is not "Electric Living: The Science behind the Law of Attraction 2.1," though understanding the concepts in that book will definitely help you grasp and apply the concepts presented in this book.

The central theme of that book is the idea that the reader can change conditions in his or her life. By thinking positively your life will turn out to be positive (you get what you want). Conversely, by thinking negatively your life will turn out to be negative (you get what you *don't* want). This idea is commonly referred to as *The Law of Attraction*.

The commonality that separated people from successful and unsuccessful seemed to be the successful person's fixation on a worthy goal which they were consciously aware of and upon which they constantly *thought*. A person attracts—hence becomes—what he or she thinks about and focuses on—because *consciousness creates*.

But the Law of Attraction is not magic—it is *science*. And, it begins with a thorough understanding of science—and knowing what it really means to *Think*. Thinking is intelligently directed and controlled consciousness. As such, there is a *reliability* associated with the process of Thinking. This is the same type of reliability we experience when we apply the scientific process. We could not rely on the scientific process unless it were intelligently directed and controlled. And so we see that real science is reliable. Real science is constant. We trust science and laws because they don't change—not because we can upgrade them every few years to sell more of the science.

We can't upgrade a physical law. We can't improve upon what is simply *true*. Granted, as time passes, understanding of the science and the laws behind it *unfold* at different rates for different people (leading to "discoveries" and "breakthroughs"), but the science and law remains the same. For example, if, for some reason, elementary science books being published today started saying entirely something different or "better" than science books published say, twenty years ago, we might question the validity of the science book.

At a certain level, the fundamentals upon which the science is built cannot change without compromising the entirety of the science. When I took science in elementary school, I learned that water was made up of two hydrogen atoms, and one oxygen atom—H_2O. I'm pretty sure that still holds true today—even though there have been any number of different and new versions of software programs that have become available. I also learned that the gravity of the earth is 9.81 m/s^2. I don't think that has changed much over the last few million years or so, and certainly not since my last book was published.

So if you bought my previous book, *Electric Living: The Science Behind the Law of Attraction,* there is no need to toss it like you would an older version of an iPhone just because a newer edition and model came out.

The message in my last book, *Electric Living: The Science behind the Law of Attraction,* is still relevant and works just as well today as it did a few years back!

Lastly, and concerning the amount of data or evidence needed to convert a skeptic into a believer, human nature often causes those who are skeptical of the validity of certain principles to look for drawn out arguments and "credible" testimonials as a form of "proof" or legitimacy. Ironically, this same human nature causes the skepticism to become more entrenched as these drawn out arguments and "credible" testimonies are presented. To the skeptic, *demonstration* is the only legitimate proof. Therefore, this book is written to best prepare the reader to go out and *do*, thereby naturally producing the demonstration which proves that *it works.*

This book is not written for the casual reader who wishes to sit back and immerse in a "coffee shop" debate on the merits. The problem with so many excellent theories is not that people don't read about them, but that they don't *do* the suggested course of action—and so the reader doesn't put much if anything *into action.* In the words of the late Wallace D. Wattles, "*An ounce of doing things is worth a pound of theorizing.*"

However, some readers *are* looking to immerse into the depths of the fundamental science and philosophy. This being the case, in addition to my previous book, *Electric Living: The Science behind the Law of Attraction*, another highly suggested reading is Ernest Holmes' *Science of Mind.* I've personally read it cover to cover, and it is a fantastic read! The subject matter itself is extremely fascinating, and though many people enjoy the studying and reading on this subject, some are not necessarily looking to dramatically alter their lives in the manner Holmes suggests unless they sincerely dedicate themselves to the *application* of the pages they read.

Indeed, there is a great difference between the reading and the doing!

I'd also like you to know and feel confident that I am "taking my own medicine," that I live and breathe the message I am prescribing. *Demonstration* is the only legitimate form of proof. Grand claims can be made by anyone. However, if the results are not present and evident in the real life of the claimant, there exists nothing more than an opinion or theory.

And so it is that the mission of the self-help author is a bit different than the mission of an author for other genres of books. As obvious as it may seem, the primary mission of the self-help author is to write a book that if applied will actually be beneficial in helping himself, as well. The result to the author must be of the same claimed result for the reader. This mission is first and foremost to accolades, awards and book sales.

Here's something else I want you to know: If you are one who needs substantial convincing or case studies before you act, this book may come across as too brief. Again, brevity is intended, and that said, I encourage you to reach out to connect with me at www.KolieCrutcher.com.

I sincerely want to meet you—and to my way of thinking, the author of the self-help book and the reader of the self-help book are always inextricably tied together. After all, I want the book to work for you, but I want it to work for me, too!

CHAPTER 1

Your Mindset—and Why it Is a Reliable *Mechanism for Success*

"Success is the progressive realization of a worthy ideal."

—*Earl Nightingale*

I'd like you to think about your definition of success. As someone who has been in the field for years, when it comes to defining "success" I note that there are basically two types of "believers."

The first group believes that "success" is somehow the result of chance or luck. Men and women in this group find ways to attribute their success or failure to factors outside of themselves and beyond their control. This group includes superstitious people as well as those who base their plans on things such as a horoscope, or, by the position of the stars, and so on. You get the idea.

The second group believes that "success" is the result of definite actions taken on the part of the individual, the foremost being "positive thinking." They also believe that positive thinking originates from within themselves and, that is within their control. They would also say that consequently, even those events that *appear* to occur by mere chance or luck, ultimately turn out to be the result of *their own* mindset.

Which group are you in?

If you are in the first group, you may struggle with the concept we're about to discuss. If that is the case, I'd invite you to be especially diligent in seeking to understand the concept I'm presenting in this book, and be bold and courageous in trying it out for yourself.

If you are in the second group, you are likely giving an honest effort to succeed. You've likely read several self-help or positive thinking books, and you pride yourself on certain habits you've developed that keep your mind "positive" and your actions "productive." Still, you may also find yourself feeling that *something* is missing, or you can't quite get to where you really want to be in life. So that's not so ideal either.

There is a better way—and that's what this book is about.

You see, as "better" as the second group seemed, the thing that prevents people in this group from completely actualizing success and "getting to where they want to be" in life, often boils down to a hazily-defined inner notion that their thinking "has an effect" on their success. In other words, they have this subtle feeling that positive thinking will definitely help them succeed—*IF* nothing too bad happens to them along the way. So while they *do* believe in the power of "positive thinking," they concurrently believe in their state of "reality" as presented to them, *more*. In other words, they do not 100% attribute their ultimate success solely to the only thing they actually control—which is their THINKING.

So is there a better way? Yes!

You see, your THINKING is not just a "strong contributing factor" to your success, or, to your failures and defeats. Your THINKING is not only an element that "has an effect" on your success or failure. Your THINKING is the sole reason for your success or failure.

Your THINKING is the sole reason for your success or failure. When you accept the idea that *anything* other than your THINKING can determine your ultimate path of success or failure, you are off-course as far as success is concerned.

In the end, we are the makers of ourselves— whether knowingly or unknowingly.

Fully accepting this reality, and responsibility, can be unsettling—if not difficult. It is much easier to think and feel that the vastness and sheer complexity of everything that goes on *around* us or happens *to* us primarily dictates our lot in life. The thought of the average person is along the lines of "*I often have zero control of all these events and circumstances that happen around me or to me so there is no way I can really control everything about my life!*"

This mindset allows the average person to "settle" or be "okay" with not becoming wildly successful because he or she will always be able to point to some unfortunate event or circumstance *beyond his or her control* that "knocked me off course." Therefore, when all is said and done, for the whatever years we have here on earth, the average person believes there is little he or she can do about the quantity and quality of the things achieved over the course of his or her lifetime—be it good or bad.

On the surface, this train of thought may seem logical. However, if we analyze ourselves for a moment, and have a bit of faith in the good of the Divine Creator (however you define that for you), we would ask ourselves a different yet very straightforward question: *Why would He allow our ultimate fate to be determined by anything we have no control over?* Free Will IS granted to mankind. But Free Will is not so much denoted by the *ability* to choose but rather, in the *power* linked with that choice. This is a most powerful concept, and with it comes a huge responsibility to become abundant in all ways.

Mankind has Free Will, yet has ultimate control over the *only* thing that ultimately attracts success or failure in life, and that is his THINKING PROCESS.

As a man of science, I can tell you that discoveries *can* be and *have* been made by what appears to be "chance," "luck," or by stumbling upon a solution that yields a beneficial or positive result. However, in order to be truly useful to the individual and humanity as a whole, *that result must be pinpointed to an underlying cause.*

It is in this manner—if the underlying cause can be accurately replicated—the desired result will surely ensue, engineered to benefit man *as he so chooses.*

The way by which the desired result is produced is known as the "MECHANISM."

Mankind has within him a *mechanism of success.* This mechanism is *attraction.* This mechanism has commonly been known as the "Law of Attraction," the notion that like attract like; we *attract* all things—be it good or bad, success or failure.

Again, whatever we attract is first and foremost dependent on the quality and power of our THINKING.

The "Attractive" Equation

While preparing for a lecture on April 21, 1820, Hans Christian Orsted made a surprising observation. He noticed that a compass needle deflected away from magnetic north when the electric current from the battery he was using was switched on and off. This was surprising because electric theory and magnetic theory had previously been thought to be *two separate and distinct* phenomena. However, Orsted's observation and subsequent findings proved—for the first time—a direct unification between electricity and magnetism. Specifically, it showed that by producing a flow of electric current *in* a wire, a resultant magnetic field would be predictably produced *around* that wire. This unification—this displayed attractive mechanism—became a force known as *electromagnetism* (more on this later).

Fueled by further research of contemporary scientists such as Andre-Marie Ampere, Michael Faraday, and James Maxwell, the understanding of electromagnetism became one of the key accomplishments in 19th century mathematical physics. Today, we know electromagnetism as one of the four fundamental forces of the universe, meaning it has always been in existence. Yet, it was not until its "discovery" in the 19th century that this ever-present force was of any practical use to mankind. In fact, our modern world and progressions in technology would not be possible without the clear understanding and application of electromagnetism.

The principle is inherently crucial in the development of automobiles, computers, telephones, and numerous other machines. However, this principle also relates to the ultimate machine: *the human mind.*

The correlation between the theory of
electromagnetism and the theory of individual
human achievement is undeniable.
This unification—this displayed attractive
mechanism—is a force known as
the *Mechanism of Success.*

Let me use the electromagnet to further illustrate this concept.
The *Attractive Mechanism* of the electromagnet is the flow of electric current around the iron core. This flow is dependent on the battery and the arrangement of the wire. In the absence of this flow, the electromagnet attracts nothing.

The Attractive Mechanism of man is likewise—and literally—the flow of thoughts around his mind. This flow is dependent on desire and the organization of those thoughts. In the absence of this flow, man attracts nothing.

Mankind is an electromagnet. As such, we can think of it this way:

- ✧ Your DESIRE is a BATTERY
- ✧ Your THOUGHTS are a WIRE
- ✧ Your MIND is an IRON CORE
- ✧ Your CIRCUMSTANCES OF LIFE are PAPER CLIPS

I'll be expanding on this throughout the following chapters. For now, an explanation I give, and one that is often quoted is: Whereas the scientist and philosopher seek to *explain*—shedding light for the sake of knowledge and discussions on the "how" and "why"—the engineer seeks the same, but for the sake of understanding and applying the *mechanism,* by which tangible *benefits* of the "how" and "why" can be brought about predictably and as desired.

In a word, doing—or more to the point, "success*ing.*"

Free Will is not so much denoted by the *ability* to choose but rather, in the *power* linked with that choice. This is a most powerful concept, and with it comes a huge responsibility to become abundant in all ways.

CHAPTER 2

Success as a Gerund:
Why "Success*ING*" Produces Results

"There is a vitality, a life force, an energy, a quickening that is translated through you into action, and because there is only one of you in all time, this expression is unique. And if you block it, it will never exist through any other medium and will be lost."

—Martha Graham, an American modern dancer and choreographer whose influence on dance has been compared with the influence of Picasso on modern visual arts

If you ask the average person to tell you what "success" is, he or she will likely say something along these lines: "having a lot of money," "a big house," "a fancy car," "an attractive partner," "an advanced degree," "a lifestyle that allows for ample time to relax, to take great vacations to exotic places, and do as I want," and so on.

This all sounds great, but in answers such as these, you also see the root of the problem. The underlying and unseen reason success eludes the masses is their basing "success" on *having a certain person, place, or thing*—as opposed to basing success on being *in the process of moving and expressing* in a certain way—a direction, so to speak. I'd like for us to explore that more. You see, the heart of this book is about "becoming successful." From the reading and applying the concepts I'll discuss, **I intend that you** *actually become successful.* And because this is the case, I am going to make a very big deal about the proper conceptualization of exactly what success *is*.

"Success"—a Gerund

What is success, *really*? What do you think it is? Most people will say, "Well, you know success is different for one person to the next; success means different things to different people." And this answer is not *wrong*—it's actually correct in a certain sense.

The idea of "success" for a young boy who desires to become a millionaire by making it to the National Football League will be different than the idea of "success" for the individual who desires to be the fastest to reach the summit of Mount Everest. But, this type of answer to the question of "what is success?" is just misleading enough to get us on the wrong path of moving forward, akin to the inadvertent and unnoticed change of switches between two train tracks that will cause the entire train (with the intended destination being Penn Station in New York City) to head in the *unintended* direction—while passengers are totally unaware of the switch. The problem of course, is that the train arrives in Albany instead of New York City.

Here's another way to think about it: If you were reading a book about feeling "blue" and in your mind your concept of "blue" was centered solely around the *color*, you would never quite grasp the understanding intended. You would technically not be *wrong* because blue *is* a color. But in the context of understanding the meaning of the intended message and subsequently taking beneficial actions, you would be "on the wrong track." It would then be easy to disregard the information as not making sense, and subsequently go about your daily business with no further thought. Then, at some point someone asks you "Why are you so blue?" If your interpretation of "blue" was about the color blue, you might respond, "I'm not blue; I'm tan!"

So that we are sure we start off (and remain) on the right track, a very important point must be made from the outset: Success is more of a *verb* than a *noun*. The connotation of this word "success" is crucially important so that the correct mental images are forthcoming and expressed as you read. For instance, in the above example the *color* blue is significantly different than the *feeling* blue. Although the two concepts are spelled and pronounced exactly the same, the mental images evoked are completely different. So with all that being said, I want you to see the importance being placed on the fact that "success" is more of a verb than a noun. And technically speaking, "success" is a *gerund.*

"A what?" you ask.

Ok, I'll admit, when I took 8th grade English, the term "gerund" made absolutely no sense. I get it *now*, but I didn't grasp that concept at the time. I understood the concept of a "noun"—a person, place or thing. And I understood that a "verb" was an action. But a *gerund* is a bit unique because it is a hybrid of the two. Technically a gerund is described as *an English noun formed by adding–ing.*

A gerund is further defined as, *"A verbal noun in Latin that expresses generalized or uncompleted action."* As applied to the concept of "success," it is the **expression of action** that we must key in on. In effect, we add our own "ing" so that we think of ourselves as "success-*ing.*"

Let's be clear. You cannot "a lot of money-*ing*," "a big house-*ing*," "a high performance car-*ing*," "an attractive partner-*ing*," "an advanced degree-*ing*," "luxurious lifestyle-*ing*," and so on.

These *things* are not in and of themselves success, per se. This is not what success *is*. These things cannot be expressed as *action*. But these things and people (nouns) are visible and they will be attracted *to you* as a result of your expressed action—**as a result of your success*ing.* That is why we assumingly attach the label of success onto those people who *possess* those things. Just keep in mind: The seen things are not the success.

It is the success*ing* that attracts the seen things.

Perhaps the best definition of success I've ever heard came from Earl Nightingale who said, "*Success is the progressive realization of a worthy ideal.*" This definition is loaded with "the action of," "the process of," "the activity of," "the doing."

Even the word "ideal" emphasizes the notion of *continuous strive.* An idea*l* is not the same as an ide*a*. *An ideal is a conception of something in its perfection.* And because a *perfect* state of anything is not attainable (we can always improve) success **is in the doing itself.** Success *IS* the doing.

Success cannot be *at* a place because you can never get *to* that place, which is a place of perfection. But the inability to reach a place of perfection is not a bad thing, *if* we understand what success really is.

Nor is success a noun. Success is not a physical person, place or thing.

This is so important because if you continue to conceptualize "success" as a noun, you will continue to "grasp at the smoke." By "grasp at the smoke" I mean you will continually grasp at that which is not attainable, or ultimately futile in its attainment. As a result, you will continually feel unfulfilled in life and not understand why. Many good, honest, hard-working people fall victim to this fate. So while it is possible to attain "a lot of money," "a big house," "a fancy car," "an attractive partner," "an advanced degree," "a luxury lifestyle" and so on, they will soon lose value and may even slip away

The "slipping away" is felt in the sense that even though you *have* those things, something will always feel "off" after some time of possessing them, if you are not being fully and continuously engaged in the proper mindset and activity in acquiring them.

For example, consider the lottery winner who gets rich literally overnight because he picked a few numbers in the right order. For many, this "found" money is the answer to all their needs and desires. Yet to many others, it is the beginning of a downfall with one string of bad luck after another, or a landslide of problems caused by having spent the money foolishly or unwisely—and we learn that the person is now not only broke, but in debt.

Why is this?

Could it be that they simply don't possess the proper mindset of seeing themselves as successful, and thus don't behave in "successful" ways that might otherwise turn their lives into a true success story?

I'll let you in on a secret. The way to tell whether or not a young individual will become wealthy—and **keep** his or her wealth for the long haul—is to ask that person what he or she would do if he won the lottery. If that person responds with, "I would quit my job and do nothing" or something to that effect, you know that whatever rewards he would "win" would soon be gone. But if his response is along the lines of, "*I'd keep doing the same thing I'm doing now,*" then you are talking to a future (and permanent) millionaire.

Success is *not* the smoke. Success is the *process, the starting of the fire.*

INCORRECT Thinking

SUCCESS is a Noun–money, house, car, degree, lifestyle . . .

CORRECT Thinking

SUCCESS is Verbal Noun (Gerund)—the in-process activity of _____-*ing.*

If you conceptualize "success" correctly—as a gerund (verbal noun)—the nouns, which is money, car, house, partner, degree, lifestyle, and so on, success will naturally follow.

The "ing" thinking puts us in the mindset of the *doing* and the *process* of and the *activity of*— which is the real definition of *success.*

Your success is wrapped up in the true expression of activity— the activity that is ongoing and can never really come to an end, because "the end" is simply a state of *absolute perfection.* Your success *is* that activity.

Success is in the *doing.*

What is your "_____ing"?

This is *your* book, and I want to encourage you to take some time to think about what that activity, that _____-*ing*—is for *you.*

Complete the following phrase for yourself.

Hi. My name is _____.

My success is _____-*ing*.

Example: Hi. My name is Kolie Crutcher.
My success is **speak***ing* / **writ***ing* / **mentor***ing* / **creat***ing* / **lead***ing*.

CHAPTER 3

The Power of "Core":
Solving the Rubik's Cube
in 30 Seconds Flat

"What's understood ain't gotta be explained."

—Dwayne Carter (Lil' Wayne)

In the 1980's a relatively new puzzle became very popular. It was called a *Rubik's Cube*. For those of you who haven't seen it, it looked like this:

Figure 3.1: Unsolved Rubik's Cube

I was a small child at the time but I remember my older cousins trying to solve it. In case you're unfamiliar with it, the Rubik's is a three-dimensional cube, with each side of the standard Cube measuring approximately 2 ¼ inches.

However, this is not a static cube. The cube has a swivel action that allows free range of motion in many directions. The sides and edges can be moved independently. In order to solve the puzzle, the object is to progressively arrange the scrambled Cube (each face having many different colors) into such a position that each of the six faces finally consisted of all the same color. In other words, each of the nine small squares that make up a face—or flat side—of the cube, had to be the same color. One face would be completely red. One face would be completely blue. One would be completely yellow, and so on with the white, orange and green faces.

If you've ever tried to solve a Rubik's Cube, you know that it can be a perplexing task of strategy and patience. So in the 80's when a twelve-year-old boy named Patrick Bossert came up with a practical way to solve it, the accomplishment shocked many adults.

So how did Patrick solve the Cube? Said Bossert, *"The Cube is an incredibly difficult puzzle to solve, but once you realize* **the center-pieces are connected,** *it does become a lot easier, because all you're doing is solving the edge-beds."*

The key in Bossert's answer is *"once you realize the centerpieces are connected."*

Patrick studied the Rubik's Cube and systematically *took it apart*. In doing so, he saw the commonality that existed with the center-pieces. In other words, he understood the *mechanism* of how it worked. By the way, Bossert also wrote a book about how to solve the Rubik's Cube, which became a global best-seller.

This mechanism is the same today as it was in the 1980's, and the rationale is backed up by Wikipedia's present-day description of the mechanics of the Rubik's Cube: *"The puzzle consists of twenty-six unique miniature cubes, also called cubies or cubelets. Each of these includes a concealed inward extension that interlocks with the other cubes, while permitting them to move to different locations. However, the center cube of each of the six faces is merely a single square façade; all six are affixed to the **core mechanism**."*

As Bossert said, *"The only way of solving the Cube is to apply a very systematic, very logical approach to it."* He did, and as a result, Patrick was able to consistently and efficiently solve the puzzle to make it look like this:

Figure 3.2: Solved Rubik's Cube

As you can imagine, the number of different combinations that are possible to get to the *one single correct combination* seems absolutely daunting. According to Wikipedia, the number of different possibilities is the number represented as "8! x 3^7 x (12!/2) x 2^{11} = 43,252,003,274,489,856,000"—which is approximately 43 *quintillion*! Daunting isn't it. As Wikipedia contends, "*If one had as many standard sized Rubik's Cubes as there are permutations, one could cover the Earth's surface 275 times.*"

So, when we hear that a young boy was able to defy such odds, and actually solve the Rubik's Cube, we are amazed.

In the same vein, we are amazed and dazzled by successful people.

From the average person's point of view, the outward signs of success (or the indicators of success as we now call them) are nearly impossible to attain. How many people do you know 1) living an interesting and engaging life filled with joy; 2) doing and accomplishing the work they feel they were destined to do; 3) residing freely in the locale—city, state, and community of their choice; 4) involved in mutually harmonious relationships based on positive qualities of love, trust, admiration, loyalty, respect and belonging; 5) having or pursuing the education and training they desire to feel competent, confident and worthy in their work; and 6) getting the quality and quantity of material riches of their own choice?

Why isn't this the case for every person on earth? Is having these and similar positive attributes not wanted by them, or do many find achieving them absolutely daunting, or near impossible?

As we look at the above six indicators, can you think of any person who does *not* desire them in his or her life? Of course, the degree, quality and quantity will differ from person to person, but the key is that something in each of us—that human element—wants these things expressed in our own unique way. For example, even the "loner" who never seems to want to be around people desires *some* form of a "mutually harmonious relationship." It may only be with one, or a handful of people. Or no one else may even see it. But his or her ability to have as few or as many meaningful relationships of the nature he wants indicates success for him.

By no means does this list detail all the indicators of success. But I think we can agree that the success we seek in our lives falls somewhere within one of these indicators or close to them. Those who have these attributes in their lives the way they want, appear to "have it all."

Those who appear to "have it all" are so few that we are often in awe when we see a person who has solved "Life's Rubik's Cube."

So the question becomes, how can we each make the *right* moves—when we have the freedom to make *any* move we want? How do we know when or how one move here is going to affect the entirety of the puzzle and either help us solve it or stymy us, or leave us feeling defeated, or maybe give up altogether?

There are so many difficulties, so many choices, so many options, and so many people. Chances of all those lining up just right are 1 in 43,252,003,274,489,856,000—or so it seems.

Many people are distracted by the scrambled outer colors and all the combination of movements in the unsolved puzzle. Few take the time and expend the effort to *look inside* and gain an understanding of the core mechanism that makes having a life of abundance easier than we think.

It's rather easy to see if all "our" colors don't match up. We see all the stuff—all the noise—going on around us. These things distract us. We allow these things to break our focus and inhibit our ability to concentrate. More often than not, we make scattered moves out of sheer desperation and guesswork. We find ourselves confused, as if we're looking at all those scrambled colors on the unsolved Rubik's Cube. We line up some things, but we move one thing and it changes another thing we *thought* we had figured out. "*How confusing,*" we think, "*I can't seem to get it right.*"

Eventually, the whole thing gets too frustrating and we give up. But to solve the puzzle, we must not become distracted by the outside scrambled colors and the noise of it all. As six-time Super Bowl winning coach Bill Belichick says, "*Ignore the noise. Do your job.*"

Your challenge is to understand the mechanism and the power at its core. Then the noise will quiet and the attributes of success will line up properly—and your life will demonstrate it as such.

If you go through life *hoping* to succeed instead of taking the time and effort to *understand* how success works, your chances of success are about the same as if you were hoping to solve the Rubik's Cube by just randomly swiveling sides, making moves by guessing, twisting here and turning there, with no real strategy. And we may reach the end of our lives with regrets and wishing we could have a chance for a "redo."

The beauty in the Rubik's Cube is the reality upon which it is built. It is so simple, yet it appears so complex to those who do not understand the hidden mechanism at its core. And you cannot "accidentally" solve it, or "kind of" get it right.

Either it's right or it's not. There is no in-between. And if you *do* get it right—well, that really speaks for itself. It was no accident.

Furthermore, you need not say a word or try to convince anyone that you understand what's really going on. Because *you cannot possibly solve the Rubik's Cube and win unless you strategize based on understanding the mechanism upon which it is built.* In case you don't remember those odds, they are 1 in 43,252,003,274,489,856,000!

One in 43 quintillion is not likely to work out very well for some of us. But this is what you're up against *if* you are just flipping around through life. A swivel here, a turn there, a lottery ticket here, looking for a "quick fix" there, but all the while having no long-term strategy, nor desire to truly *understand* the puzzle of your life—of which *you* are the center. We must seek to get to the important part.

Do not seek the outer appearance but instead seek the inner operation that ultimately controls the outer appearance.

The scrambled Rubik's Cube can be solved in less than thirty seconds—*if* you know what you're doing. On the other hand, there are people who have had Rubik's Cubes that they've been playing with off and on, since the 80's—never solved.

Do not mistake movement for progress.

Do not mistake movement for progress.

CHAPTER 4

Attraction Action:
Why You Get What You *Attract*

When we see a successful or famous person, our initial thought is along the line of, "Wow! What he or she is doing really works." Whether it is a business person who makes an astonishing amount of money, an entertainer or artist who consistently tops the charts and wins awards, or an athlete who wins multiple championships, most of us marvel at those successes. They are uncommon. We see people who are "success stories" covering the magazines and being interviewed on television. They are the talk of radio shows and camera crews follow them around. We clamor for their attention and seek their autographs. They are held in such a high place on the totem pole because we perceive *something* about them is different. *Something* they know is different. *Something* they are, is different.

That "something" is just that they have solved the "puzzle of success." As a result, success showers them with all the spoils and riches and fame they want.

We see all those indicators of success and we think, "If *I* could just get success to work for *me*." In our rush of excitement caused by the glitz of their indicators of success, our famous heroes inspire us to make another run at success for ourselves.

We figuratively dust off that old Rubik's Cube of our life that we've been half-heartedly wishing to solve for years. But as we swivel and turn, making this move and that change, we are again quickly reminded that solving this puzzle is "just too darn hard" (which is why we put it on the shelf years ago), and so we resign our fate to living vicariously through those "lucky few"—the winners, our heroes, who *did* solve it.

Catching a glimpse of them in person or attaining an autograph will have to suffice as a reasonable facsimile of the excitement we would have felt if we had "made it." After all, you can still *rent* a Ferrari for an hour or two. But while one person is fanaticizing about the successful person's Ferrari—a new invention that brings riches, a famous book, new toy—you name it, the successful person is fanaticizing about the expression of activity he or she habitually engages in, which attracted the Ferrari (or a new invention, famous book, or new toy) to him as an *afterthought.*

An example would be the likes of Bill Gates, Steve Jobs, Kobe Bryant or Michael Jackson. I've recently listened to interviews given by all of them. If you've ever heard these people talk (especially during their younger years), listen carefully. They invariably speak in terms that express the process of improving what they do, rather than talking about the material things they have. Bill Gates is a billionaire and can likely buy as many Ferraris as he wants, which is one reason people are initially awed by him. And of course we are attracted to his philanthropic lean too, the Bill & Melinda Gates Foundation—a grant-making foundation that supports initiatives in education, world health and population and community giving. Certainly this is awe inspiring too!

But the point here is that we must keep in mind that *the things seen are always attracted by a power that is unseen.* It is highly likely that Bill Gates doesn't want another Ferrari even though he can easily afford it. It is likely, though, that he will continue engaging in the activity that produced them. Like most "successful" people, it's the activity, not the Ferrari, that propels him.

Because we rarely see ourselves capable of achieving even our own desires to the heights of Bill Gates, Steve Jobs or Tony Volpentest—we tend to view becoming successful as something that is *hard, maybe impossible.*

But attaining success is "hard" only because we "listen to the noise."

If you are focused on the core mechanism, the doing, the indicators will appear naturally.

The Attractive Mechanism

Understanding the mechanism of the Rubik's Cube helps us understand the *importance* of looking for the inner mechanism that controls the outer demonstration. But the dynamics of our very own life needs to be understood by grasping the mechanism of something more representative of mankind, and that something is the *electromagnet.*

Why?

Because the electromagnet has a mechanism that displays itself as attracting—*attractive*—*just like mankind!*

Both the electromagnet and people have an *attractive mechanism.* As I explained earlier, the *attractive mechanism* for people is literally the flow of thoughts around one's mind. This flow is dependent on desire and organization of those thoughts. In the absence of this flow, the mind attracts nothing.

The *attractive mechanism* for people is the
flow of thoughts; in the absence of this flow,
the mind attracts nothing.

CHAPTER 5

Are You Having *"Thoughts,"* or Are You "THINKING"?

"The victim mindset dilutes the human potential.
By not accepting personal responsibility for our circumstances,
we greatly reduce our power to change them."
—Dr. Steve Maraboli

The *Attractive Mechanism* of mankind is literally the flow of thoughts around his mind, this flow dependent on desire and organization of those thoughts. Man's conscious *relationship* to this flow determines the quality of his life. There are three possible relationships:

1. ABSENCE: In the *absence* of this flow, a person attracts nothing. In this case, the individual is basically dead or in some vegetative state where there is no brain or heart activity, and no flow of thought.

2. IGNORANCE: In the *ignorance* of this flow a person is extremely limited, as he or she "attracts" only that which is already around him—for good or bad.

3. CONSCIOUSNESS: In the recognition and *consciousness* of this flow, a person can attract that which he or she aspires to—in spite of the "limitations" of his present conditions and circumstances—which may appear to contradict his aspirations. Concerning

consciousness, awareness is the starting point. *Thinking* facilitates the mastery of the consciousness, as the individual's conscious relationship progresses from mere awareness to true belief.

In other words, Thinking is intelligently directed and controlled consciousness.

Levels of the Consciousness Relationship

Because the 3rd type of relationship (the consciousness relationship) is where we want to be, its discussion warrants a closer look. There are five levels of the consciousness relationship. They are 1) awareness, 2) interest, 3) knowledge, 4) understanding, and 5) belief. Keep in mind that these levels are not necessarily distinguished by hard and fast boundary lines, but rather they blend into one another as do the colors of the spectrum. The change is a gradual one, and although the process of progressing from one level to the next may not be noticeable from one day to the next, as long as you are truly Thinking, rest assured that progress is being made.

Thinking is the "vehicle" that moves you from one level of consciousness to the next, just as surely as "studying" moves you from one grade level to the next in school. And just as in school, life presents us with "tests" (opportunities), and our responses show our level of consciousness. A person who has just begun to undertake the process of Thinking will be only at the first level (the level of Awareness). In life, he or she is okay, as long as things are relatively easy. But he will be able to solve those more challenging issues (those which require Understanding or Belief) no more than a first grader will be able to solve a math problem intended for a 4th or 5th grade level student. But some day, he will, if he continues to put forth the effort. Sadly, many people are "held back" in life, simply because they don't engage in Thinking. We see them all the time. "Why are they not further along?," we say to ourselves. And although it may not be politically correct, we all remember the kid in 7th grade who was always goofing off instead of studying. He stood out because he was 14 years old, while everyone else was 12.

THINKING is a progressive process. THINKING is intelligently directed and controlled consciousness. Diagramed, it would look like this:

Awareness → Interest → Knowledge → Understanding →Belief

LESS THINKING   MORE THINKING

Earlier I told you that:

✧   *Your THINKING is not just a "strong contributing factor" to your success or failure.*

✧   *Your THINKING is not just something that "has an effect" on your success or failure.*

✧   *Your THINKING is the sole reason for your success or failure.*

What IS *Thinking?*

Here's what I mean by THINKING. In every moment you are awake (and even just before falling asleep) you have *choices* as to where you "place" your consciousness. Having this Free Will you direct your five senses and consciousness to any place you choose. The most efficient and effective way to place your consciousness somewhere or onto something (and keep it there) is to be engaged in *doing an activity*.

As you are doing the activity you are controlling your consciousness onto that activity. If your consciousness was not controlled onto the activity, you could not be doing the activity with efficiency or effectiveness. Hence, the *more focused and engaged you are into the activity* the more directed and controlled your consciousness is.

The *more focused and engaged you are in an activity,* the more directed and controlled your consciousness is.

This is a very important point to bring up for those who feel "thinking positive thoughts" without any associated progressive actions can somehow magically attract the lifestyle they desire. The recent popularization of the "Law of Attraction" is partly due to its perception of "ease and inaction" commonly associated with the term "thinking."

This diluted connotation of "thinking" is not the type that powers the electromagnet that is *you*. It is too weak to provide attraction.

Yes, while you are idle and simply imagining (daydreaming), you are "conscious" and somewhat aware of the things you want. But that is only pointing you into the direction in which you must now *walk* and progress with your consciousness. Being aware is only the starting point.

Your consciousness is best controlled by the doing! Void of the doing, your consciousness of a thing is easily swayed to something else. It is *un*controlled. In this state, your consciousness exists in a cloud, just like those clouds in the comic books when a character has a thought or idea to himself. And it subsequently will blow away just as easily as a cloud by something—anything—else that enters your mind.

So we see that it is the doing that "locks your consciousness in" so that consciousness has that crucial characteristic of being controlled.

The goal is to develop consciousness from shallow awareness, to deep belief. *You cannot develop that of which you have no control.* Again, when there is no action taking place, there is no real control of the consciousness.

Hence, we use the lowercase everyday general term "thinking" to describe the common, low intensity consciousness of something that is easily swayed and not controlled. This is the daydreaming or fantasy of a better life (the comic book cloud), without any actions to back it up. It's what is meant when a person says, "Hey, you know, I was *thinking* about starting my own business." But since the person never progressed forward from the mere initial awareness, all he or she ever did was *think* about it, and that cloud is soon blown away.

You have no doubt heard the phrase, *"An idle mind is the devil's playground."* When you are idle and not involved in concentrated and focused action, it is much easier for you to begin randomly "having thoughts." These are the uncontrolled flow of thoughts *not* of the nature you desire. They are akin to a guest who just walks into your home, uninvited. *Having thoughts results in a completely different experience than THINKING.*

A person who is merely "having thoughts" has an experience like that of a person taking a shower, yet having no control of the flow out of the spigot. Being at the mercy of the flow, he or she may soon experience the sensation of freezing because the water is too cold or he may experience the pain of being scalded because the water is too hot. In the absence of control, the chances of experiencing a warm shower of just the right temperature lessen. On the other hand, a person who is THINKING takes the shower and enjoys a warm soothing experience because he or she has control of the flow.

Thoughts are constantly flowing, so we must constantly ask ourselves, *"Am I having thoughts, or am I THINKING?"*

Thoughts are constantly flowing, so continually ask yourself, "Am I having *thoughts,* or am I THINKING?"

Contrasted to the lower-case "thinking" associated with idleness and lack of control while "daydreaming" or "having thoughts," we use the uppercase "THINKING" to describe the controlled, highly focused consciousness that accompanies doing and being engaged in the activity. By this definition, we can easily see how a person fully concentrating and engaged into the *activity* of playing a chess match—for example—has a more controlled consciousness of chess than someone who is simply reading a book about chess. Likewise, the person reading a book about chess has a more controlled consciousness than a person who simply has a fleeting thought of *"It would be nice to learn how to play chess."*

Intelligently Directed

In addition to being "controlled," THINKING is also "intelligently directed." Intelligently directed implies that before you "lock in," *you* make the choice on where you want to place your consciousness. You have Free Will to choose for yourself. So, if you are locked in to doing something you really don't want to do, your choice has not been made intelligently. If this is the case, you won't stay fully engaged and focused for very long.

> To the extent that you are fully engaged in activity that is focused onto your own personal choices, is the extent to which you are THINKING.

Ignorance of the Flow

A good number of people fall into the ignorance of the flow, because they do not even possess the simple awareness of the flow of their thoughts. Let's explore this a bit more.

Every day, all around, vast numbers of people find themselves in unfavorable circumstances, while at the same time ignorant of the flow of their thoughts. This is the reason for that "life is not *fair*" phrase. For example, a child born into a negative situation will automatically be subjected to negative thoughts with no real say-so in the matter.

Negativity is passed on to him, and can become a way of thinking for the child, as well. As a result, "bad things" might then be happening *to* him, much like a sleepwalking person who accidentally breaks a glass in the middle of the night, yet has no recollection of his actions.

We cannot literally "see" thoughts and feelings, so it is easy to take them for granted. And it is even more of a challenge to condition yourself to actually believe that the thing that you *can't* see is the thing in control of everything you *do* see!

Overcoming the "Unfairness of Life" — and Taking Responsibility, Nonetheless

It is your *fault?* No. But it is still your *responsibility.* Why? Because the mechanism is what it is—regardless of the circumstances that initially set it into motion. This is where we must overcome the "unfairness" of life and learn that we must ultimately take responsibility. *With great power comes great responsibility.* And just as surely, *with great responsibility comes great power.* They work hand in hand. You were given this power, but you must be responsible for it at all times! Otherwise it can destroy you. It is unfortunate that most people must "hit rock bottom" before they step back and take a look at *themselves.* An individual can only change by objectively looking at himself in terms of his flow of thoughts. The great news is that when you do accept the responsibility— regardless of how "fair or unfair" circumstances appear—you have the power! *Even as a child, you had this power, and were using it.* And it is highly likely that—unless you were born into very favorable circumstances—you were unknowingly using this power in a self-damaging fashion instead of a self-favorable fashion.

Understand: You don't have a choice to say, "*You know what, I don't really want this power. I'd just like to be normal.*" This is not an option because there is no such thing as a "normal" human being. You are powerful and amazing beyond comprehension! You're like Spider-Man—once bitten by the spider, you've got the power! So in actuality, those Marvel characters are closer to the truth of our human nature than we realize.

By simply being able to read these words and ponder how they relate to you, you are already in possession of this power. Ask any five-year old if he'd like to be Spider-Man and he'll gladly accept, excited to use his powers, with no fear. "Who'd want to be *normal?*" he thinks. But as we get older we fear *ourselves*, and we slowly want to be "normal" or "like everyone else." But again, the conflict for the adult is that he goes through life trying to blend in and be the very thing he is *not*: normal. The adult is not normal. The adult human *is* a powerful super hero. And the price we pay for *not* using our power is that we fail to achieve the greatness of who we are, and of what we can become. Thus, in spite of our "okay" lives, we often feel like a failure, or that we didn't make of ourselves what we silently knew could have been—"if only."

I won't go into all the details of the "miraculous human body"—the heartbeat, the breathing, the regenerative skin, muscles, and so forth because they are so much a part of you that they don't make you *feel* powerful. You've always had these things, so they give you no sensation of power. It's akin to being a flame and someone trying to tell you that you are hot. As the flame, you would be a bit confused. "Hot? What is that?" Your inclination is to honestly deny the fact that you are hot simply because you don't know what "hot" is. You are simply *you*. You "is" hot. Hot "is" you.

Where there is absolutely no separation—no inequality—there can be no relative sensation.

Because the flame *is* hot, the only way the flame could experience the sensation of "hot" would be if it were somehow able to separate itself from itself—which could never really happen. At the point of separation, it would then cease to be "itself." But if it *could*, the flame could somehow separate its consciousness out, and then somehow move closer to its former self. Only then, as it moved closer, it would be able to experience the increase of temperature and the sensation of "hot."

The previous example is impractical for the human for one simple reason: *You can never truly experience anything from any perspective other than your very own perspective.* I'm not talking about having *empathy* for another person. Empathy is when something happens to another person and you truly feel either good or bad *for* them. Even in the case of actually feeling a certain way because of your closeness to that person or "putting yourself in their shoes," you are still experiencing the feeling from your own point of view. You are casting your point of view or feelings onto their situation as it relates to *you*. There is no way around this truth.

There is one thing that is impossible for a human to do. When referring to himself, he cannot hold the feeling of "I am" and "you am" at the same time. In other words, he cannot think "I am" *for* another being.

You don't use your power because you can never get away from it long enough to *see* it. You don't sense it. *Where there is absolutely no separation—no inequality—there can be no relative sensation.*

The only clue of your power is your ability to construct the thought of "I am," because outside of this ability, what *you are* is basically insignificant. Take a look:

Element	Symbol	Percentage in Body
Oxygen	O	65.0
Carbon	C	18.5
Hydrogen	H	9.5
Nitrogen	N	3.2
Calcium	Ca	1.5
Phosphorus	P	1.0
Potassium	K	0.4
Sulfur	S	0.3
Sodium	Na	0.2
Chlorine	Cl	0.2
Magnesium	Mg	0.1
Trace elements include boron (B), chromium (Cr), cobalt (Co), copper (Cu), fluorine (F), iodine (I), iron (Fe), manganese (Mn), molybdenum (Mo), selenium (Se), silicon (Si), tin (Sn), vanadium (V), and zinc (Zn).		less than 1.0

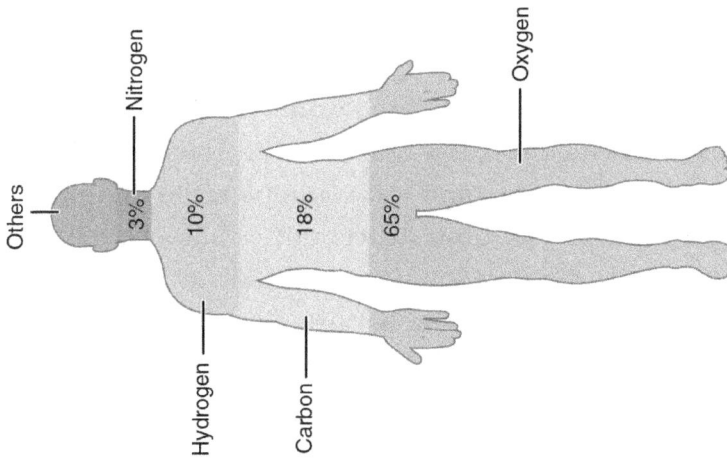

Figure 5.1: Elemental Composition of the Human Body (by OpenStax College–Anatomy & Physiology)

Figure 5.1 is a chart showing the elemental composition of the human body. Taking a look at what "you are," you can see that almost 99% of the mass of the human body is made up of six elements: oxygen, carbon, hydrogen, nitrogen, calcium, and phosphorus. From this representation, it is clear that if the totality of all those elements were "over there" in a pile, *unaware of its own existence,* it would have little monetary worth.

If one were "shopping for" these common elements in a chemical store, they could easily be purchased for mere dollars. As a matter of fact, these elements are so common that a shopper would only need about *one dollar* to purchase the amount of these elements comprising the average human body.

Any of us could look at that pile of elements and say, "You are practically worthless." And we'd be absolutely correct . . . *until,* and *unless* that pile actually *heard* the comment, now aware that someone thought of "it" to be worthless. At that point—at that point of awareness of *being*—that pile has a concept of "*I amness.*" In other words, it is a being. And ironically, the mere ability to know that its considered worth is one dollar by another being is what makes its worth unlimited.

Now, whatever that *something* is that allows that pile of elements to simply know its considered worth to be more or less a few dollars only, and also know of itself to be Mary, John, Mike, Sally, and so on, has been, and will continue to be the topic of lectures, debates, and sermons for centuries. But whatever that something is, it is the base creator of all that is. In its *absence,* nothing else could actually exist. Because even if something else *did* exist (as in the case of the pile of elements just sitting "over there" with no awareness of itself), if there is no one around that can think "I am," then there can be no concept of "*you* are."

"*You* are" implicitly contrasts "I am." "You are" gives form to what "I am" *not*. The moment you think "you are," you admit that you have also conceptualized "I am."

So again, nothing can exist without a concept of "I amness," as all that we see out there in our world—the "you areness"—is always in relation to our very own point of view. We know of it, even if it cannot know of itself, because we can know of *ourselves*.

This concept is so subtle, yet so important. I suggest reading the above by yourself, and in a very quiet place so you ponder the concept in your imagination, and read it again until it makes sense. It may take some time to grasp the point, but it's worth the mental energy and activity you will expend thinking seriously about the essence and nature of your very own being.

If you don't understand *you*, you can't really understand anything else, because everything else only has meaning in relation to *you*.

Again, our "human" conflict is that the very thing that makes it possible to have any and every thing we want in life is so common to us—so *near* (and "near" is not even the proper word, as "nearness" implies *some* separation) to us, that it is as if it didn't even exist. *We can't lose it, but few use it.* And we can't see it in anyone else because you can never experience "I am" from another person's perspective.

We can never experience "I am" from another person's perspective.

CHAPTER 6

What You
and an Electromagnet
Have in Common

"Iron which is brought near a spiral of copper wire, traversed by an electric current, becomes magnetic, and then attracts other pieces of iron, or a suitably placed steel magnet."

—Hermann von Helmholtz

The start of this chapter is strictly basic physical science, and not all that different than what you may find in any elementary school science book. As a matter of fact, the following information regarding the operation of the electromagnet is available free online in the public domain.

As stated earlier, the *mechanism of success* is simple. To demonstrate the simplicity of the mechanism by which an *electromagnet* operates, I've included a very basic demonstration. Please take a few minutes to view this demonstration at:

www.mechanismofsuccess.com/buildelectromagnet

The following depicts the components of a simple electromagnet.

Simple Electromagnet

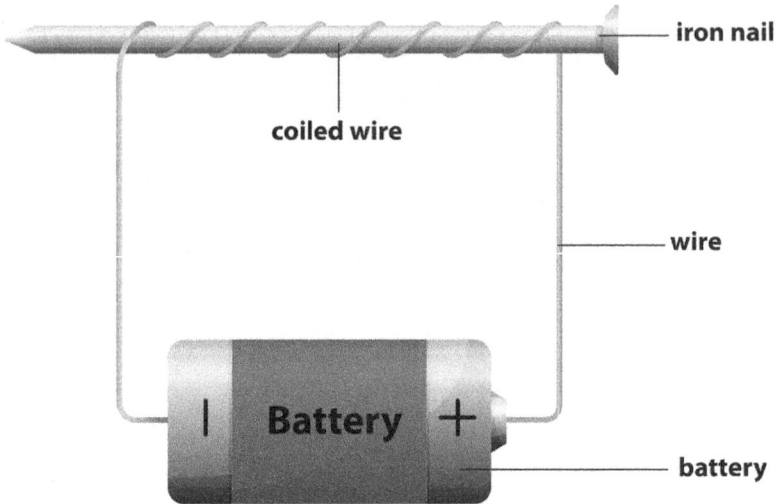

Figure 6.1: Simple Electromagnet

As seen in Figure 6.1, the simple electromagnet consists of three basic components:

✧ Battery

✧ Wire

✧ Iron Core (Iron Nail)

Furthermore, the strength of the attractive magnetic field depends on the following factors:

✧ The number of coils around the iron core;

✧ The amount of electric current flowing through the coils; and

✧ The type of core material (iron in this case).

And here is where we want to look closely at what is really going on to produce what we call an "electromagnet." The physics is quite simple but if you've never seen it before, you may want to read it through carefully a few times. Also, writing down your own notes and simple calculations on these pages helps the process of understanding.

STEP 1:

When an electric current (I) runs through a wire, a magnetic field (B) is generated *around* that wire, as depicted in Figure 6.2.

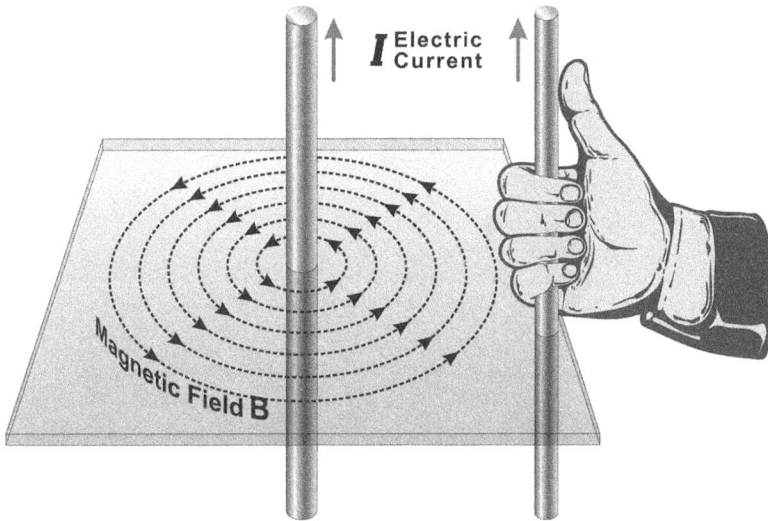

Figure 6.2: Magnetic field generated around single wire

NOTE: The magnetic field "wraps around" the wire in the same way your fingers wrap around the wire if you were to hold the wire in your right hand, *with your thumb pointing in the direction of the electric current flow.* This is known as the *right-hand rule.*

STEP 2 (FIGURE 6.3)

Because the magnetic field (B) around a single wire is relatively weak, the magnetic field strength can be multiplied by *coiling* the wire, which concentrates the field in the center.

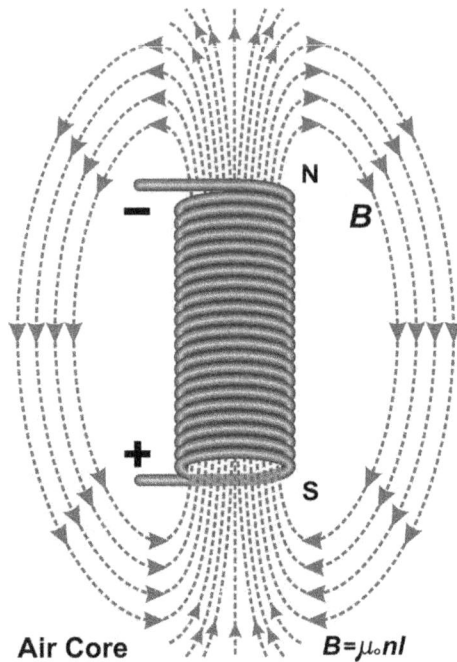

Figure 6.3: Coiled wire concentrating the magnetic field

STEP 3 (FIGURE 6.4)

Placing an iron core within the coils of the wire has the effect of amplifying the already concentrated magnetic field. This further intensities the strength of the magnetic field (B).

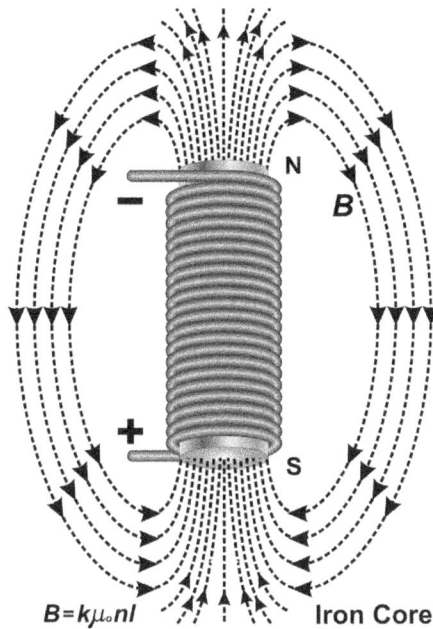

B=kμₒnl   Iron Core

Figure 6.4: Iron core intensifies magnetic field

Summing up the above figures in mathematical terms, you will notice the equation $B=ku_0nI$. This simple equation describes the strength of the magnetic field:

B	strength of magnetic field produced
k	relative permeability (used when core is non-air substance, such as iron)
u_0	permeability of free space (air core)
n	turn density (number of coils per meter length of iron core)
I	electric current (in amps)

In other words, increasing any of the terms k, n, or I on the right side of the equation will produce a stronger magnetic field. The u_o term is a constant, and will always remain the same because it is the permeability of free space or air.

Of note: the relative permeability (k) varies from substance to substance. For magnetic iron, the value of k is around 200. This means that placing an iron core inside the coils produces a magnetic field strength *200 times stronger* than if there was simply air within the coils.

As an example, let's say that we take a copper wire and coil it 25 times around a 6-inch (0.1524 meter) iron nail. Then, we connect the ends of the copper wire to a battery so that a 2 amp (A) electric current begins to flow. What is the strength of the resulting magnetic field measured in this electromagnet we have just produced? Well, according to our equation to determine magnetic field strength, **$B=ku_o nI$.**

It is also helpful to know that magnetic field strength (symbolized as B) is measured in units called *Tesla* (T).

Now it is just a matter of plugging in values for the right side of the equation in order to determine the value of the magnetic field, B.

k = 200 (if iron has a relative permeability of 200)

u_o = 1.2566370614 x 10^{-6} T(m)/A (because the permeability of free space is a constant)

n= (25 coils/0.1524m) = 164.04 coils per meter

I = 2 (because the electric current flow is 2 amps)

Because all of our above numbers are already given in terms of meters (m), amps (A), and Tesla (T), all we have to do is plug in the values to get our final answer in Tesla.

B = (200)(1.2566370614 x 10^{-6})(164.04)(2) =0.0824 T

So, our *electromagnet* will produce a magnetic field of 0.0824 T. And just what does that mean? Well, the strength of a typical refrigerator magnet is 0.003 T. So our electromagnet is roughly 27 ½ times stronger than your typical refrigerator magnet.

Now, as long as we have a flow of electric current (as in Figure 6.1, with the battery connected) within the wire, we have an **electromagnet.** The important part to keep in mind is that none of this is possible without the fundamental reality of STEP 1: *When an electric current (I) runs through a wire, a magnetic field (B) is generated around that wire.*

The other steps are just the taking advantage of this simple natural phenomenon!

From the video demonstration I suggested you watch, and from the diagrams shown in this chapter, we can see that we may now *test* the attractive strength of the electromagnet by introducing another component. This testing is crucially important because *we cannot see the magnetic field*, even as the electric current is actively running through the wire. We can only know of the magnetic field's presence by taking note of the magnetic field's *effect* on other materials.

These materials are technically not part of the basic electromagnet, but rather can be used to show the effects of the magnetic field produced. Paper clips, iron filings, or some other metal that is attracted by the magnetic field indicate the strength of the electromagnet.

So now, we have four very basic parts at which to look. We have the three basic components of the electromagnet, and we also have the material, which indicates the attractive strength of the electromagnet:

- ✦ Battery
- ✦ Wire
- ✦ Iron Core (Iron Nail)
- ✦ Materials to attract (paper clips, iron filings, other metals).

You'll notice in the video demonstration that the mere presence (or the improper arrangement) of the components does not activate the attractive mechanism and pick up paper clips. There are two specific actions that must be taken to make these components operate as a true electromagnet. (1) The wire must be coiled multiple times around the iron core. (2) The connection to the battery must be made. Once these actions are taken, the attractive mechanism of the electromagnet operates automatically, *as indicated by the drawing of the metal paper clips.*

NOTE: It may not be presently clear—the reason for studying the mechanism of the electromagnet in an effort to understand the mechanism of our very own individual achievement. Do not be discouraged. The understanding will unfold over time.

Here's the great news right now! As it pertains to the individual, you already have all three of the basic components as they relate to the simple electromagnet! Every human has all of these components already "there."

- ✦ Battery = DESIRE
- ✦ Wire = THOUGHTS
- ✦ Iron Core = MIND
- ✦ Materials to attract (paper clips) = THINGS/CIRCUMSTANCES OF THE LIFE YOU DESIRE

Here's an example of how it could play out:

- ✧ DESIRE = To start a Graphic Company

- ✧ THOUGHTS = A company of my own will allow me to use my talent and allow me to arrange my work to fit my energy and the needs of my young family. Designing your logo, writing out your business plan, setting aside a small amount of money for your future business, practicing your designs

- ✧ MIND = The mind is already there, working out the ways and means of "making it happen." You no more have to bother or worry the mind to perform than you have to bother or worry on breathing or pumping your heart. The mind operates most efficiently when relaxed and expectant. Faith is all that is required here—knowing that the mind will (in ways never revealed to man) take care of the "how", because we have now provided the above "what" (the **DESIRE** and THOUGHTS)

- ✧ THINGS/CIRCUMSTANCES OF THE LIFE YOU DESIRE = Opportunity, seemingly "out of the blue" to present your business plan to the right person to fund the company such as a "chance encounter" with a CEO the world's foremost graphic company. This is the real beauty of life—the *surprise* events, circumstances, meeting of people—that are almost surreal when they happen. When you look back at how circumstances unfolded to "bring to you" that material equivalent or personification of your DESIRE and THOUGHTS, you realize the MIND was indeed hard at work, although its "pull" was not evident until that very person you needed to meet, magically appeared.

Now, concerning the "paper clips," you may not see them in your present circumstances, by now you should be getting an idea that you can *arrange your three basic components so that those things and circumstances of life you desire are attracted to you.*

So in looking at ourselves and our lives in particular, we can begin to view ourselves as a "human electromagnet," no different that the simple electromagnet. Go ahead and get comfortable with it:

Hi, my name is: _____) I am a human Electromagnet.

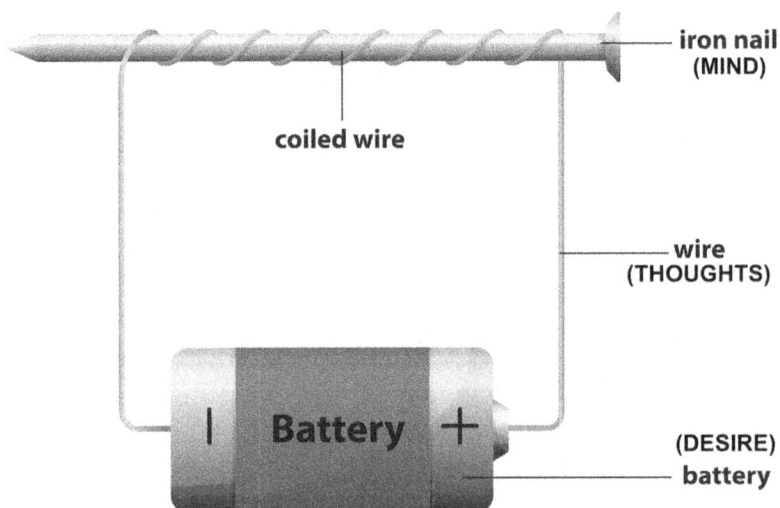

Figure 6.5: Human Electromagnet

IMPORTANT: This "human electromagnet" version of you as shown in Figure 6.5 is not the "you" you see when you look into the mirror. *You cannot see this version of you with your physical eyes.* However, it is just as real. And you must see this version of yourself with your *mind's eye.*

Now, just as the case with the simple electromagnet, the *mere presence* of these components does not automatically activate the attractive mechanism and attract to you the life you want. *All of us* have (1) some desire, (2) thoughts and, (3) a mind. But we must understand how to properly *arrange* these components of ourselves in order to activate the attractive mechanism and begin attracting the things, people, circumstances, and yes—"luck"— we desire to have. Otherwise, we attract nothing. And therefore, this lack of proper arrangement of your basic "mental components" is the only reason any man cannot have the life he wants. *He is ignorant on how to organize and arrange the free components of himself he was given at birth!*

Again, just as is the case concerning the simple electromagnet, there are two specific actions you must take, so that the attractive mechanism "kicks in" and operates beneficially in your life:

✧ YOU MUST ORGANIZE YOUR THOUGHTS.

✧ YOU MUST CONNECT TO YOUR DESIRE.

In other words, you must (1) coil your wire and (2) connect your battery. If you cannot organize your thoughts through discipline and connect to your real desire of what you love to do, you will attract the very same thing as the unorganized components on the simple electromagnet—*nothing.*

If you study the life of any individual who has "attracted success," you will see that he or she (1) organizes and controls his own thoughts, and (2) is deeply connected with what he loves to do. That's it!

So from our list of three basic components, and the materials to attract, we now narrow our focus down to only two, because those are the two that require **effort on our part** to activate the attractive mechanism. Therefore, the details of those efforts to properly assemble the components are covered in the next two chapters in this book.

Battery: INNATE DESIRE—CONNECTING TO YOUR POWER SOURCE

Wire: DISCIPLINING YOUR THOUGHTS

We won't even discuss the iron core component, because *you already have a mind.* But that mind is simply not attractive as you wish it to be yet. And in the same vein, we don't need to further discuss the materials to attract—the paper clips—because *all that "good stuff" is already out there.* It is just not in *your* possession yet.

These are the "indicators of successing," I discussed earlier in this book.

Iron Core—MIND (you already have a mind)

Materials to attract (paper clips)—*things/circumstances of the life you desire* (no further discussion; those things are already "out there"—just not in your present possession).

Before we continue to these last chapters relating the attractive mechanism of the electromagnet to the attractive mechanism of your life in particular, we must be extremely cautious not to mistake *simplicity* for *ease.* By mistaking simplicity for ease, you will either become misled, or disregard the information as inapplicable. Regarding the first case, *do not be misled* to believe that the process of arranging your components to cause the proper attractive mechanism will occur *without effort* on your part. Concentrated effort is surely required!

Regarding the second, *do not disregard* the attractive mechanism due to its simplicity. In other words, the natural tendency of the reader may be to disregard the attractive mechanism of the electromagnet because it is "too simple" (and maybe "too good to be true") to apply to your "difficult" life. But, *everyone's life is not difficult.* Some people have an "easy" life. Therefore, if your life is consistently "difficult"—if you are not attracting the good things, people, circumstances—*it could very well be that it is difficult because you don't yet truly understand the simple mechanism by which life operates.*

Keep in mind that even the most basic machines that we take for granted today would have been extremely difficult to operate or even comprehend in the 18th century. Moving in an "automobile" or flying in an "airplane" or talking on a "telephone" would have been difficult to the point of being "impossible" in the 18th century.

Why? Because this simple mechanism of electromagnetism was extremely difficult to make practical use of until the 19th century, just because no one knew of it! This is despite the fact that the mechanism itself has never ever changed.

Electromagnetism is one of the four fundamental forces of the universe. It is just as simple today as it was in 1820, as it was since the beginnings of the universe. It is not like the mechanism of electromagnetism started off very complex (and thus *un*usable to man) in the beginning of the universe, and then somehow billions of years later the mechanism became simple—and thus useable by man—in the year 1820.

The mechanism that was mind-boggling to the world's great scientists 200 years ago is the same mechanism demonstrated and explained in elementary school science fairs today.

In general, the mechanism is forever simple. In particular, the difficulty or ease with which that simple mechanism can be *used to benefit man* depends on man's *discovery and understanding* of that simple mechanism.

Stated another way, ignorance of the most simple mechanism makes those processes that *could* utilize that unknown mechanism (if known) appear to be extremely difficult. The ease in operating the machine *appears* to change based on man's discovery and understanding of the *mechanism.* But the mechanism—in and of itself—is, and has always been simple.

Electromagnetism is one of the four fundamental forces of the universe.

CHAPTER 7

The "Innate Desire":
Connecting to
Your Power Source

*"To go wrong in one's own way is better
than to go right in someone else's."*

—*Fyodor Dostoyevsky*

From our brief study of the mechanism of the electromagnet in the last chapter, it's fairly easy to see how by taking away the battery, we take away the entire attractive power of the electromagnet. The battery is the source of power for the electromagnet. Taking away the battery results in the loss of electric current flow. A weak battery results in a small or negligible electric current flow.

As it pertains to individual achievement, *our desire is what moves us.* A person with a burning desire to accomplish a thing can think of all sorts of ways and possesses all sorts of energy to get it done because he produces a great magnitude of thought flow. Therefore, we must learn to properly connect to our desire. Attempting to accomplish something that you have no real desire for is akin to connecting a dead battery into any device or machine—nothing happens.

In matters of interpersonal relationships, to find out what a person *really wants* or *desires*, is always key—and sometimes challenging. Most people don't really understand their desire, and therefore can't consciously communicate what they really want as they journey through life. But in our own self-study, it may be even more challenging to decipher what we really want of ourselves.

For our purposes here, it is important to go deeper than what initially comes to mind when we think of our "desires." A person may "desire" an attractive partner, or "desire" a sports car, or "desire" the money and power to influence and improve our own life and as well as those around us.

Desires certainly fuel our pursuits. However, using these desires to fuel us may prove of value for only a short period of time. As we learn, grow, change—and even age, our desires can change. As a result, we must constantly modify and bring clarity to what we specifically desire. The sports car drooled over in your 30's may not excite you when you're in your 80's. A promotion you so vigorously sought when in your 20's may not get you to move across the country in your 50's.

So that's one factor.

Another is that living within a certain community or locale can influence our desires. For example, if you live by the beach or the ocean, you desire a kayak, or jet skis, a boat, or fishing gear. If you live in an urban community, you may wish to own memberships to a workout facility, or to certain clubs, or own a cabin in the mountains for weekend get-aways. Again, the point being, that we are influenced by our surroundings more than we may realize.

So the average person may continually change his or her mind about what he or she desires without ever really understanding why they feel as such.

But imagine if we rev up to live by the water, and shortly thereafter, we then move to an urban setting, where maybe we live in a smaller apartment or condo. Then we marry or have a family, and so we are again looking for change. Being constantly in a mode of change can leave you feeling excited—until you begin to tire of the change, and wish to "put down roots"—which is another way of saying you are also looking for a core of something more permanent, or constant.

In the main, things, places, situations and people excite us for a short while, but after a while, we may find ourselves searching for some *other* desire to energize us—and so we turn to our *Innate Desire*—a desire that is deeply rooted within our psyche. We loved and enjoyed it before "society" prescribed what we "should" want, love and enjoy. Our Innate Desire sort of guides us, even though we may not be able to conceptualize its importance to us or describe to others why exactly it appeals to us. It may subtly reveal itself in that you preferred the outdoors to being inside, or that you preferred your alone time to crowds, or, that you preferred being social more than you enjoyed being alone, and so on.

We can better access this if we reflect back to early childhood and remember what we truly loved doing—a time in your life when you made choices based on an inner desire, choices not swayed by what other people thought of those choices.

All of us, as we grow and mature, become much more concerned about what *other people* think of us. This can be both good and bad. If we become much more concerned about what *society* thinks of us than we are about with what we really want, then we hand over the steering wheel of our life to the opinions of others who are but mere passengers.

It's natural that we are shaped by others. We hold within a desire to be liked by others, and thus are influenced to fit in; peer approval, regardless of age, is real. What is important is to not let go of the "who I am" within.

The word "selfish" usually has a negative connotation. But if you really want to be able to help other people in a meaningful way and for the long term, you must focus on that internal "who am I" and not lose it—regardless of the desire to please others. This "focus" allows you to *develop you*. Otherwise, you have nothing to truly offer anyone else. The all-star great Michael Jordan said it best: "*To be successful, you have to be selfish, or else you never achieve. And once you get to your highest level, then you have to be non-selfish. Stay reachable. Stay in touch. Don't isolate.*"

The Societal Dilemma

Here is the societal dilemma—the societal bribe—faced by far too many. Society is outwardly structured to provide law and order *for the group as a whole*. So while there may be no inherent predisposition of society to disregard or hurt the individual (a debatable topic), the mere fact that society must function first and foremost to provide law, order and stability for *the group as a whole*, necessarily means that the *individual's* desire must take a back seat and be of *secondary importance* in a smoothly operating society.

Therefore, as we get older and more influenced by society, we are more influenced by the built-in desire of society and the other people of that society, as opposed to our own individual personal desire. Society seems to reward those who "fit in," "get along with others," "don't cause problems," because that is what benefits the whole of society. Unknowingly, we become willing (and even eager) to trade in our unique deep desires, ambitions and aspirations in exchange for the common, watered-down "desire" of fitting in. It's similar to taking a bribe.

As a very young child, we valued our individual uniqueness.

There is nothing wrong with a society working to benefit the whole of people rather than the individual. As a matter of fact, we should be grateful that rules are in place to keep order and "even the playing field." In societies where this is not the case, there is lawlessness and people suffer. The purpose of a smoothly operating society is so that there exists the opportunity to stand apart and achieve—even if most people don't know how to take advantage of those opportunities.

The Abby Moment

I remember being 4 and 5 years old and naturally doing and saying *whatever I wanted.* This was not done in a disrespectful way, or in a manner that was malicious or with bad intent. Rather, it was done simply because I felt the natural freedom to do and say truly what I desired. I was happy because my actions were not burdened by having to take into consideration the opinions of others. My thoughts and actions did not pass through the societal filter, and were not influenced by the "societal bribe."

Looking back, my first remembered dealings with this societal filter (unknown to me at the time) came in kindergarten. One day, I told this girl in my class—Abby—that *she looked like a witch.* I didn't tell her this to be mean but because it was around Halloween time and we were coloring witches in class. The witches were not "ugly" or "disgusting." And to me, Abby just looked like one of the witches we were coloring, so I told her. "Hey Abby! You look like a witch." The teacher overheard me and I got in trouble.

Abby cried, and I was confused. I got in trouble because what I said "wasn't nice" and I made Abby cry. I had disrupted the "classroom society." I thought it was strange that I got in trouble because I was only telling what I thought to be true. As a matter of fact, I didn't even know how to lie. The strangest aspect of the whole situation was that I actually really liked Abby. As a matter of fact, I remember liking everyone in my class. I was 5 years old! At that age, I didn't know that what I thought, felt and said was supposed to be of secondary importance to *how* what I thought, felt and said made those around me *feel*. I didn't know that what I thought, felt and said was expected to "blend in" in such a way that it didn't disrupt society.

Now, I think we would agree that as adults, we can't recklessly and maliciously go around mindlessly doing whatever we want to do with absolutely no regard. As we get older, our ability to act out can cause more societal damage than it can as a very young child. The goal is not to create a disruptive society. I mention the *Abby Moment* only because you may be able to find your *innate desire* most easily by searching back to a period of time *just before* you began being so influenced by the societal norms. The trick is to go back in your memory and feel that spirit of unfiltered honesty of your childhood, without dredging up the "brutal" aspect of being an uncensored adult that unnecessarily makes others uncomfortable.

And then again, many find it when they get to the work force. For example, a person starts work in a position that requires multiple skills and in completing them over time, the person discovers he likes working with "numbers" and has a real knack for it. And, he learns that he isn't much suited to be a team player, either. Time on task over time confirms and solidifies all this for him, and a year later he decides to pursue a degree and become a CPA and go into business as a sole practitioner. He is someone who now often says "I love what I do; I love my life. I'm very happy now."

It's not my intent in this chapter to provide the tools that determine your talents, aptitudes or innate desires, though I would encourage you to discover these for yourself, because they can help you confirm what you probably already know about yourself, and so you can make informed decisions in pursuing goals that lead to your doing what you were "meant" to do. There are a number of good books on the subject and you can quite easily find tests and tools to help you take a look at "YOU." That said, as I've been saying all along, it's also a matter of developing a keen sense of *self-awareness*; know yourself. For example, early on I could tell that I had a natural affinity for words and a curious mind. Reading and discovery was always just as natural to me as breathing. Books were always around me, and my earliest memories of books was an automatic interest to read them, and the play of words and their meaning brought me enjoyment, comfort, and delight. The innate desire within me for learning, language and discovery demanded to be heard. How did all this manifest for me? Like this: I never remember a time in my early life when I *couldn't* read. I never remember having to "learn" how to read.

There is much sovereignty in identifying and connecting to your innate aptitudes and talents: they are a pure source of power for you—and help you live "close to the bone," to stay true to "who" you are and what you are meant to be and do. In the "noise," pressures, and bribes of life that steer us to "fit in," following this inner power source can help you also stand apart.

I never remember any difficulty, hardship or burden associated with words, books or writing. I loved reading more than I liked going outside to play. And this was long before I started kindergarten. So when I did start kindergarten, I thought it very strange that the teacher would stop what she was doing and take notice when I just started picking up books and reading them.

I thought it very strange when the teachers from the 2nd and 3rd grade classes would come and listen to me read books. The teachers would get their lunch and actually come to my class to eat while I read. A short time later, I remember my mom telling me that I was going to be advanced directly into the 2nd grade; no 1st grade for me. I still didn't really know why, but okay!

The deep desire to do what you do, simply for the love of doing it proves trustworthy and provides freedom for you throughout life—even if you lose touch with it for a short time. And here's the great news: Even if you "lose touch" for a while, it never really disappears. So you may notice it "popping up" again later in life, and in the experiences that bring you joy—or pain. The beauty (and the difficulty) in connecting to your Innate Desire is that no other individual can point it out to you. No one can absolutely tell you "Hey, that's it." But here are some questions to consider that will help you in the process of connecting for yourself:

- ✧ Do I enjoy working with people, or machines, or with animals?

- ✧ Do I prefer working with others, or working alone?

- ✧ What bothers me? (a clue to the type of problems you were meant to solve)

- ✧ What kind of people do I habitually choose as friends or partners?

- ✧ Do I prefer being indoors or outdoors?

- ✧ Do I prefer working with numbers or working with the people?

- ✧ What Causes most stir me, to that I readily donate time and effort to?

- ✧ Do I prefer to travel often or spend most of my time in one place?

- ✧ Do I prefer to go to the party or plan the party?

- ✧ Am I a "morning person" or "definitely not a morning person"?

- ✧ Do I prefer to communicate via telephone or by text/e-mail?

- ✧ What profession would I choose if all paid the same amount of money?

- ✧ If I had exactly 10 years remaining to live, how would I spend that time?

Taking some time to think on these types of questions as they relate to you will help you connect with your Innate Desire. Your Innate Desire is a trustworthy source of power because ultimately you can't effectively move *on your accord* without it. Because we all share this society, we all will be influenced to a certain degree by factors beyond our control. However, if you cannot connect to your Innate Desire, your actions will always be indirectly controlled by someone else, to the point where you feel habitually unhappy and unfulfilled.

The goal is to be inner-directed. So you must develop the courage to do it on your own (not by *yourself*)—regardless of how others *appear* to be moving. It is your lifetime: don't sleepwalk. LIVE your life. Don't hesitate to march to the beat of your own drum.

These words by E.E. Cummings ring true: "It takes courage to grow up and become who you truly are."

CHAPTER 8

Disciplining Your Thoughts:
The Great Iron Hand

"I practice as if I'm playing in the game. So when the moment comes in the game, it's not new to me. That's the reason why you practice . . . that's the effort. So when you get to that moment, you don't have to think. Instinctively, things happen."

—Michael Jordan

The human mind is a very abstract concept. In other words, we cannot actually describe or look at the "mind" of an individual in the same way we can describe or look at the individual himself. An individual "John Doe" may be described as being 5'10," with black hair, brown eyes, slim build, a tattoo on his right forearm—and display countless other visual and sensory attributes. These attributes can be used to identify the individual John Doe, apart from any other individual. An artist or photographer can replicate the likeness of Joe Doe so that there is no mistaking his identity. However, after looking at Joe Doe, and being able to easily describe him, draw him, or photograph him, we would be a bit perplexed if we were then asked to describe the *mind* of Joe Doe.

The artist would not know where to start. The photographer would likewise be confused. But, in spite of the absence of a description, we cannot deny the fact that John Doe does indeed *have* a mind. The dilemma arises in that the extreme difficulty in seeing or describing the mind does not negate its existence.

Having said all that, if there *did* exist the ability to somehow look at the minds of the most attractive people—and by "attractive" I mean possessing attributes such as being truly deeply happy and accomplished—we would clearly see that their thoughts follow a certain arrangement and direction. There is an ordered and organized way which follows a certain pattern. Their thoughts are wound around their mind into a certain concentrated pattern that facilitates this ordered and organized way. Here's the power in that:

✧ **A *tightly* wound mind has a strong attractive force.**

✧ **A *loosely* wound mind has a weak attractive force.**

This chapter explains what we mean by a "tightly wound" vs "loosely wound" mind.

End results are generally easy to visually comprehend. For instance, the bank balance and material assets of a rich man are easy to visibly contrast to those of a poor man. However, the causing mechanism that precedes and attracts the resultant financial status in each is usually very difficult to *see*.

For this reason, and because we humans are overwhelmingly visual creatures (yet unable to "see" the mind), it is absolutely imperative that this book translates the unseen causing mechanism into the mechanism that *can* be seen. Otherwise, a very powerful attractive force is flat out overlooked, simply because that attractive force cannot be seen or otherwise detected by any of the human senses.

Earlier in this book, we looked at the attractive force of the electromagnet and the corresponding materials it attracts. So we can more easily see the causing mechanism that attracts steel, iron and other metals to it. Furthermore, we will see the *correlation between the arrangement of the wire that carries the electromagnet's electric current and the quantity of things attracted by the electromagnet.*

I reiterate that the strong electromagnet has a tightly wound electric current-carrying wire arranged around the iron core.

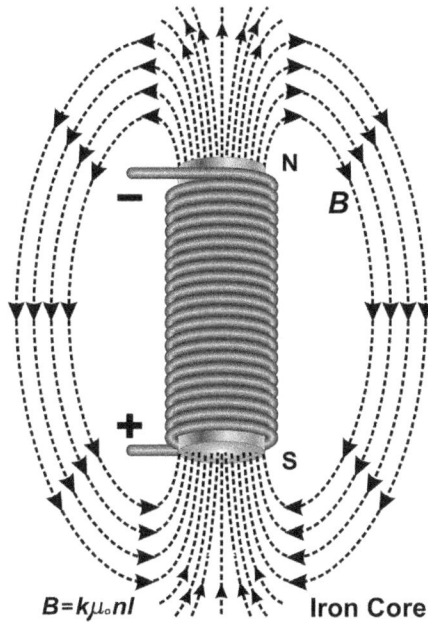

$B=k\mu_o nI$ **Iron Core**

Figure 8.1: (same as Figure 6.4): TIGHTLY coiled arrangement. The concentrated flow of the electric current-carrying wire around the iron core in a strong electromagnet.

This chapter stresses the importance of the *arrangement—* the organization—of the wire. Looking at Figure 8.1, this spiral arrangement dictates the specific path of the electric current as it flows. Remember, in an *electro*magnet the flow of electricity (electric current) is necessary to create the attractive force of the magnet. But this flow cannot be haphazard or unorganized. The flow must be orderly, organized and defined into a certain concentrated pattern in order to create a useful electromagnet. The electricity flows along the path of the wire in the same manner that water flows along the path dictated by the arrangement of a garden hose. Hence, it is easy to see how the wire arranged in the Figure 8.1 will cause the electric current to flow in a very distinct, orderly and repetitive manner. And it is the sum of this very distinct, orderly and repetitive flow of electricity that gives the attractive strength to the electromagnet.

Organized repetition and concentration of the flow is the key. In the Figure 8.1, there are twenty-four or so coils through which the electric current flows. In general, the more coils of wire wound (and hence through which the electric current can flow) around the iron core, the stronger becomes the attractive force of the electromagnet. All things being equal, an electromagnet with only twelve coils would be only half as strong as an electromagnet with twenty-four coils. However, an electromagnet with forty-eight coils would be twice as strong as one with twenty-four coils.

In terms of the mind of the human, the flow of thoughts (and feelings) is *always* taking place within you. And again, what this chapter stresses is the specific *arrangement and concentration* of that never-ending flow. You cannot allow those thoughts to just flow any way they please without your consent and without some form of organization. You must *discipline* the flow of your thoughts. All of us *have thoughts*. But very few of us *Think*. *Thinking is intelligently directed and controlled consciousness.* Stated another way, Thinking is simply the disciplined flow of thoughts and emotions.

Thinking is intelligently directed
and controlled consciousness.

Thinking is simply the disciplined
flow of thoughts and emotions.

Thinking is the natural result of practiced acts of discipline. When you have attained a disciplined flow of thoughts, those thoughts flow in the predetermined manner in which you want. Your thoughts will naturally flow through your "mental wire" along the concentrated coiled path, and produce an attractive force in your life, just as it does in the electromagnet!

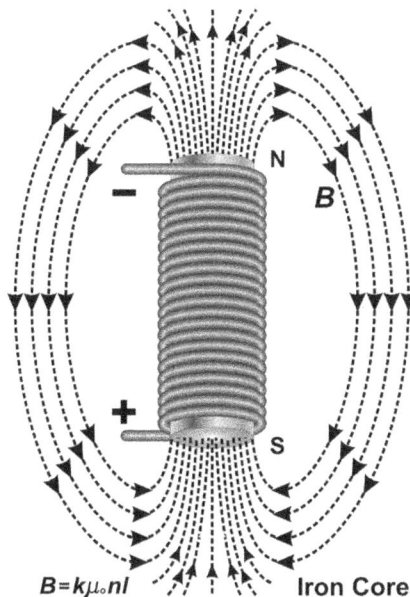

Figure 8.2: TIGHTLY coiled arrangement. The concentrated thought flow and "magnetic field" around a strong attractive mind

It is no mere coincidence that the flow of thoughts around the mind of the strongly attractive individual follows the same arrangement as the flow of electricity around the iron core of the strong electromagnet. Keep this image in mind as you continue reading this chapter.

"What's On Ya Mind?"

When I was a kid, my dad would habitually, and almost as a greeting, ask me "*What's on ya mind?*" As a child, it's difficult to grasp the true meaning of certain phrases and questions brought to your attention. But because this was the question he most frequently asked me, and because he didn't ask about a variety of other trivialities, I got the impression that this was the question that carried real importance.

I never knew exactly how to answer but because the question was always asked, I always pondered it. Many years later, I know that this was the correct impression. Why? Because the simple fact is this: If you concern yourself with thinking about what's actually "on your mind," you will gain the ability to *control and direct* what's on your mind. In other words, you will be able to *control and direct* your thoughts and emotions.

We must get into the habit of *thinking about what exactly we are thinking about.* When we look at the electromagnet, we see that how the wire is organized around—or *on*—the iron core, dictates the attractive force produced by the electromagnet. Likewise, how our thoughts organize around—or *on*—the iron core of our mind dictates the attractive force in our lives. Truly "*what's on ya mind?*" is the only really important question. If we can answer this question, the answers to all the other questions will eventually reveal themselves.

"What's on ya mind?" is the only really important question; If we can answer it, the answers to most all the other questions reveal themselves.

One of those others questions takes the form of a slight tug inside that asks something to the effect of "What is the purpose of life", or "Why am I here?" Whatever your answer and however you feel that you deeply want to spend your time here on earth, one thing is certain:

You must go through some form of development in order to get onto the path you aspire to be. And ultimately, the tool that you use to get on that path is your very own mental machinery. That's right. The very thing you can't see is the only thing that can get you any and every thing you *can* see! The very thing you can't locate is the only thing that can get you where you want to be. Money can't get you there. Other people can't get you there. Another person can "help you" or "do something for you," but no one can THINK *for* you!

The goal, the struggle and the very essence of life itself is to get your thoughts to flow around your mind in the same manner that the electric current flows around the iron core in a strong electromagnet. This arrangement of flow automatically creates a mind with a strong attractive force. And this phenomenon is what has been commonly known as the "Law of Attraction."

Getting to this attractive point is the holy grail of life itself. But it does take time to master the process! The results seen by the outer world don't show until after much time and effort of consistent mastery of the inner world of thoughts. So in the quest for quick fame and riches, and by not wanting to put forth the necessary time to develop the mind's organized repetitive thought pattern, we will accomplish and attract nothing of note.

This is due not for lack of *ability* but for lack of *persistence* in sticking with **one thing** long enough so that your thoughts of that one thing have tightly and repetitively wound its many dominating coils around the mind. Remember: More organized repetitive coils, equals a more attractive force.

All of the great "self-help" teachers and philosophers—from Jesus Christ to Napoleon Hill and others dedicated to helping people "become better" or "live a better life"—have stressed the *same message* stated in varying ways. And that message is simple: *We become what we think about.* And, because of this universal truth, they likewise all (again, in slightly different ways according to personality) stress the same skill as being the first and most imperative duty of man: *We must control our thinking.*

What cannot be denied is the fact that, each repetition, when you take the time and effort to specifically choose the nature of your thoughts and feelings, you take that electric current-carrying (thought-carrying) wire of your mind, and coil it. You systematically direct it. You can have as many coils as you want. As seen from the Chapter 6 and reiterated in this chapter, the more coils around the iron core, the stronger the electromagnet becomes—*automatically.* And pertaining to you, the more coils around your mind, the more attractive you become—*automatically.*

The "Law of Attraction" seems to work like magic to those seeing the results in your life. However, what is described in this chapter is the unseen science—the discipline—that actually *causes* the attractive magic that others don't see. The law is not something one can master by casually reading a book or learning a short-cut technique. Those looking for a "secret" will never find it because it remains hidden within the repetitive coils of disciplined thought practice. And, the accompanying time and concentrated effort of disciplined thought practice cannot be bypassed.

Remember: The audience sees the effortless "magic"; the magician understands the effort of the disciplined science. After time, effort and discipline is replaced by "habit force." This habit force pulls from within the subconscious of the individual, and now he or she is able to instinctively do things and make things happen *without* consciously thinking.

It's as though someone else—some perfect force—was in control of your body, freeing your conscious awareness to just be there, and enjoy the show of greatness.

The Loose Ease of Neglect

The opposite of discipline is neglect. Being neglectful is easy, because all you have to do is *not* put forth the effort of disciplining your thoughts. The undisciplined neglectful mind has a current-carrying wire akin to the following:

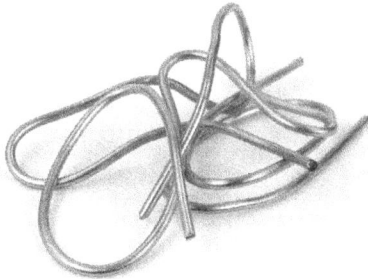

Figure 8.3: LOOSE Uncoiled arrangement of the electric current-carrying wire, which symbolizes the undisciplined, neglectful mind, and very weak to non-existent attractive force

The undisciplined mind *reacts* to his environment and circumstances instead of *creating* an attractive force that causes his environment and circumstances to conform to him. Looking at the wire in Figure 8.3, and applying what we have learned about the electromagnet, how can this type of messy configuration create any attractive force?

A flow of electric current in this wire will be all over the place, changing direction with no apparent order and never able to follow a path of tightly wound and concentrated coils. If you were to place an iron core in the middle of this mess and connect the ends of the wire to a battery, you would not have an electromagnet, but rather, a bunch of useless iron and copper wire. Whereas in the previous example shown in Figure 8.1, the wire had many tightly wound coils, this has few if any.

In the same manner, if the wire in Figure 8.3 is symbolic of what carries the thoughts around the mind of the neglectful person, it is easy to see how the mind will attract mostly confusion and a disarray of things they *don't* want. Those undisciplined thoughts flow in whatever direction the wind blows them, yet leaving the person still ever responsible for those thoughts.

Many times, he or she pays the price for the stray and tangled thoughts, blind-sided when hit by "bad luck" and "misfortune." Yet if the unfortunate incident(s) in his life had a string attached to it, the person experiencing them would see that some equivalent negative feeling and misguided thought were attached, likely still operant below the surface. This negativity likely slipped in while discipline was off-duty. Discipline keeps the good thoughts in and the bad thoughts out.

The disciplined mind maintains the thoughts it desires regardless of the environment and circumstances. If a change in thoughts is desired, he *responds* based on the conditions and circumstances he desires and aspires to. This response is a deliberate change in the flow of thoughts, not simply an out of control reaction.

Thinking is not *easy*. It requires much effort and discipline to consistently have thoughts flow in the direction of your choice and volition, as opposed to the direction dictated by outer circumstances. We as human have this ability.

Thinking is a difficult skill to master, but not because it is complex. It is innately a simple process.

Mankind: "Warm-Minded "

In elementary biology we were taught that *cold-blooded* animals (such as frogs and fish) take on an inner body temperature dependent on the outside environment temperature. Cold-blooded animals do not have the ability to maintain their inner body temperature. So if it gets cold outside, a frog's inner body temperature will drop, and the frog will become sluggish and inactive due to the low body temperature. On the other hand, *warm-blooded* animals (such as mammals and humans) maintain their body temperature regardless of the outside environment temperature. Therefore, warm-blooded animals can still remain active even if the temperature drops and it gets cold outside.

For humans, our body temperature maintains 98.6 degrees. If the temperature is 20 degrees outside, the warm-blooded human body will automatically attempt to maintain an inner temperature of 98.6 degrees—or very close to this figure within a degree or so. For this reason, a human body temperature just a few degrees above or below 98.6 indicates a problem. 95 degrees or below generally indicates the problem of hypothermia (too cold), while 99.5 degrees or above generally indicates a fever (too hot).

Although there is no hard and fast set cut-off temperature, the human will generally not survive if the body temperature drops below 70 degrees or rises above 108 degrees Fahrenheit.

The degree to which the outside environment conditions affect the conditions on the inside can be applied when dealing with the mind as well. The "cold mind" (or neglectful mind) will take on the thoughts and conditions of its outer environment. The cold mind will change based on the bleak outer conditions and negative thoughts given off by other minds. The "warm mind" (or disciplined mind) will maintain its own thoughts *regardless* of the bleak outer conditions and negative thoughts given off by others.

While there are many warm-blooded animals, there is but one "warm-minded" being and that is mankind. Animals don't have the ability to alter their environment by controlling their flow of thoughts. And because animals don't have the capacity to Think as does man, animals instead have certain strong *instincts* to help them deal with and blend in with their predetermined environment.

No matter what the animal does, he cannot appreciably change his position in life, like man has the ability to do. Man is not supposed to weakly conform to his environment and circumstances. Man is supposed to boldly make his environment and circumstances conform to *him*. This is the purpose of the mind of man.

When you "set a goal," or define your life mission, you are basically taking advantage of the fact that you are warm-minded. Whatever your goal is, it serves the same purpose that "98.6 degrees" serves in being "warm blooded." You figuratively "set the thermostat" and the outer environment changes and adjusts to the level set.

The crucial point here is that, being warm-blooded is an automatic unconscious feature of the human body. As humans, we don't have to put forth any thought or effort to maintain a constant body temperature of 98.6 degrees.

On the other hand, being *warm-minded*, man has the *ability* to maintain his thoughts. Yet in order for the ability to become an automatic response, **discipline must be practiced over a period of time.** If you discipline your mind, you will soon find that when the outer environment conditions of life get "too hot" or "too cold" for everyone else, you will *maintain* an air of positive thoughts and feelings and keep moving. The "cold-minded" people will shut down, taking on the negativity and bad conditions around them. They will become as sluggish and hopeless as the frog who can barely move in the winter.

Unless a person truly **uses** his or her mind and ability to THINK, he is relegated to the lower plane—that of an animal, meaning:

- ❖ Whatever general status he had at birth, he will rise no higher.

- ❖ His life revolves around basic needs of eating, sleeping, reproducing and procuring shelter. And these will seem to be a struggle.

- ❖ After death, he leaves no substantial evidence of his existence. Nothing is passed down for later generations to build on concerning either material assets or useful knowledge to procure material assets. Those who come after him, must start off at zero, and must struggle in the same way for the basic aforementioned needs.

However, the man who does not use his ability to think is in many ways *worse off* than the animal. At least the animal has strong instinct to guide it. Man does not have strong instinct; he was designed to THINK. Therefore, most men find themselves in the perpetual "concrete jungle," hungry and hopeless, and feeling ill-equipped to secure the basics to survive. At least if he were an animal, he would not be so hungry. For he would at least have those strong instincts to ease the burden of securing food. Animals use their speed, great power, sharp teeth, honed senses, camouflage, or just the ability to find food growing; animals don't need money to eat.

The ability to think, yet *not* do so, also causes man the lasting sorrows of regret, fear, and so on. Again, animals—since they don't innately possess the ability to Think—can't really misuse this ability and destroy themselves, as does man. Animals don't lay awake at night, regretful of their deeds. The undeniable proof of man's ability to Think is the unyielding sorrow that follows him as a result of living in a way of *not* Thinking. Animals don't possess the firepower of intelligently directing and controlling their thoughts to shoot life down and make it yield all the pleasure and riches they desire.

Humans possess the firepower but *by not using it,* effectively turn their guns onto themselves—unknowingly destroying themselves in the process. With great power, comes great responsibility.

It is a better life to be an instinctual animal, than an *un*thinking and undisciplined man!

Recognizing Discipline

Perhaps the greatest insights one individual can give another is the opportunity to witness his discipline in action. It is important to recognize and respect discipline when you see it. But true discipline is so rarely ever seen that most people never notice it. So what does discipline look like? Well, if we are looking at the electromagnet, we can easily see the many organized tightly wound coils. But in people, you won't see the "tightly wound coils" wrapped around the discipline-minded person.

But you will notice that the discipline-minded individual makes things *look* easy—*things that are hard for everyone else.* People see your nice home, fancy cars, and life of joy and abundance. It *looks* easy. But they themselves can't *attain* it. People see you doing something with great proficiency. It *looks* easy. But they themselves can't *do* it.

Take professional sports for instance. When you watch Stephen Curry of the Golden State Warriors shoot a basketball, he makes it *look* easy. His accuracy and proficiency of shooting—especially from long range—is unlike anything the NBA has ever seen. The ease with which Curry shoots the basketball—and the inability for opponents to stop him—makes the casual fan feel as though he could go out and shoot like that. The same is true with watching the NFL's Odell Beckham, Jr. catch footballs with one hand for the New York Giants. "Wow. That looks *easy!*" the casual fan thinks as he watches the game on television.

In both cases, it's not just the actions, but the *ease* with which these professional athletes appear to perform those actions. It makes the onlooker almost feel that they could do it too. *But unless and until you put in* the disciplined practice, probably *you can't.*

Remember, each disciplined shot in practice is a directed coil of the wire around the mind. Each disciplined one-handed catch in workouts is a directed coil of the wire around the mind. In the actual game, as the ball is in the air, the crowd is screaming and your opponent is coming at you full speed, you don't have time to consciously consider positioning all the elements of your body to make the shot or catch the pass. You just go! But now when you go—you flip the switch—the flow is going to move along the arrangement that you set up in years of practice and workouts—*automatically*.

The flow cannot move in any other direction because you have already deliberately set the course and arrangement of the wire through which that flow must follow. The result is the pinpoint accuracy of shooting demonstrated by Steph Curry and the spectacular one-handed catches of Odell Beckham, Jr. *look easy*. It's as if the basket that Curry shoots into has some type of magnet that attracts the basketball. It's as if the hand that Odell Beckham, Jr. uses to catch the ball has some type of magnet that attracts the football.

What's Done in the Dark

We've all heard the phrase, "What's done in the dark, will eventually come to the light." But it is usually meant to refer to bad deeds. However, this phrase is music to the ears of the disciplined-minded. Why? Because **the bright lights reveal the discipline of the night.** The "night" in this case is when no one is watching, cheering, congratulating, and showering you with adoration. As Ray Charles would say, "*The night time is the right time.*" And the reason is simply because *discipline is forged "at night" and "in the dark"*—when no one is watching. It's easy to get excited when everyone is cheering and watching. However, you must get yourself hyped not for the game, but for the practices and workouts *before* the game. If you do, the results of the game—whether the game is basketball, football or life—will be automatic.

Is everyone going to the NBA or the NFL? No, of course not. We all are born with slight differences and predispositions that make us unique. So as you take inventory of yourself and reconnect to your Innate Desire, you will notice that this wire will have a slight tendency towards some activity. It is up to you to consciously direct that slight bend into a distinct and tightly wound coil that can only be forged through years of discipline. Eventually, it will be your time to shine. And when you do, your shine will be natural and automatic. But you must put in the disciplined work when no one is watching.

Remember: The bright lights reveal the discipline of the night.

The Great Iron Hand

It is very helpful to visualize discipline as The Great Iron Hand, purposefully coiling the wire around your mind.

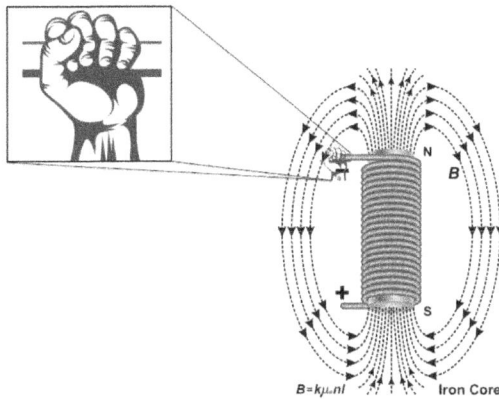

Figure 8.4: The Great Iron Hand coiling the "mental wire" around the mind

And each time you take the effort to genuinely think, feel, and act in the manner that you wish yourself to be, The Great Iron Hand is forming another coil in your mental wire. It does take great effort in the beginning. Most people live a reality that is far from what they wish to be. So "feeling and acting as if you were already the thing you wish to be," sounds crazy. But as time passes and you continue to practice this discipline, you will notice things slowly changing for the better in your life.

You will notice that those things you have disciplined yourself to think of start "popping up" when least expected. Why? Remember, the flow of thoughts never stops. And since you have now disciplined the flow around the mind and created a great number of coils, the flow that never stops is now traveling in a manner that creates the attractive force strong enough to "bring in" the nature of those thoughts! This is the working principle of the electromagnet. This is the working principle of the mind.

Over time, it gets to the point where you couldn't be *un*successful even if you wanted to! This is what rapper Curtis "50 Cent" Jackson meant in his song "I Get Money" when he said, "*I used to couldn't do good, now I can't do bad.*"

NOTE: When you are first starting out, it is important to keep your grand ideas, thoughts, and plans to yourself! Because thought energy cannot be seen, it is extremely easy to wastefully dissipate—especially through talking. But don't worry, because you'll have plenty of time to tell everybody of your great plans. You just have to show them first. Furthermore, most people simply don't know *how* to Think, and will (intentionally and unknowingly) tend to dissuade *you* from Thinking. Even those loving friends and relatives who "mean well" will inadvertently interfere with "The Great Iron Hand" coiling your mind by throwing in *their* point of view as to how you should do things. Just stay the course. Hold on to your desires. Believe and achieve.

The disciplining of the mind is a journey you must make alone.

There is only one YOU. So if you can't use *your* own mind, what's the point of even being here? Some people worry that they need other people's input and advice because they might "get it wrong." Don't worry about being "wrong." If you "get it wrong" by truly making your own decision, you can easily "get it right" the same way.

Once you get mentally strong enough (many tightly wound coils) you can get help from people to help facilitate your accomplishment, without allowing them to change your own mind (uncoiling). Then you can start sharing your ideas and plans with others—accepting or rejecting as you please.

If you never see the real purpose of discipline you will never practice and develop real discipline. And unless you forge mental discipline all your mental energy, great thoughts, plans and ideas, are weak. They may actually be "great ideas," but because they lack the proper direction, concentration and arrangement, they go towards attracting nothing but false hopes and empty promises.

This is simply the way the attractive mechanism of the electromagnet operates. *This is simply the way the attractive mechanism of the human mind operates as well.* In closing, here's something to ponder: If you pass a real electromagnet (with tightly wound coils) over a pile of unknown materials, it will attract and pick up only the metal—iron, steel and the like.

All of the other useless paper, rubber, wood, trash, and so on, will be left behind!

CHAPTER 9

You Are YOU:
Attracting the Life You Want Is Destined

"Be still, and know that I am God."
—Psalm 46:10

With all this talk of the *mechanism* of success, you may now be thinking of yourself as some type of . . . *machine.* I'll admit, this is not a bad way to picture yourself. According to Wikipedia, technically a machine is "a tool containing one or more moving parts that uses energy to perform an intended action."

Many of us don't like to think of ourselves as machines because we think of a "machine" as being cold and heartless—lacking feelings and empathy. While this is largely true, it only holds true for the lower level machines. And what do I mean by "lower level" machines? Well, the creat*ed* is never greater than the creat*or.*

All machines created by man—no matter how complex, technically advanced and dazzling they appear—are only a poor knock-off of the ultimate machine—*man.* And this "human machine" *does* have a heart and feelings; it *can* think and feel independently of an outside operator. This "additional feature" (found only in the human machine) is *exactly* the reason man is greater than all other machines he creates. Stated another way, man's ability to think and feel does not *exclude* him from the category of machines; it simply puts him *atop* the category. It is this difference—this additional mechanism (the flow of thoughts) within the machine—that allows man to operate *himself* as he so chooses.

The ability to intelligently direct and control this flow of thoughts (Thinking) allows the human machine to reign as *the ultimate machine.* This is the mechanism that sets him apart from all other machines, and able to dictate his own fate. Remember, the Attractive Mechanism of man is literally the flow of thoughts around his mind. This flow is dependent on desire and organization of those thoughts. In the absence of this flow, man attracts nothing.

In today's technology-driven era, we are so accustomed to using our machines to make our lives more convenient and to express ourselves. iPhones, MacBooks and all different kinds of machines are personalized around our individual lifestyles. It is no accident that many people feel "lost" without their smartphone or favorite tech gadget. And I think we all can agree that if you want to really know about a person (how they truly express themselves), look through the machines and gadgets they habitually use—their MacBook Pro, their iPhone, and so on. And we go to great lengths to figure out how those machines operate—knowing they will reciprocate with a certain level of convenience and allowance of self-expression we expect.

But sadly, too many of us don't know how to operate our "machine-self." As a result, we make our lives *more* difficult (as opposed to more convenient). We *stifle* our uniqueness (as opposed to expressing ourselves).

The literal concept of being a *machine* is likely jarring, but if you could for a moment, imagine yourself to *be* an iPhone—

fresh out of the box. Would you spend all day using yourself to dial up people you *don't* desire to talk to? No, of course not. As a matter of fact, when we no longer want to have anything to do with a person, what do we do? We *delete their number from our phone.* We *block their number from our phone.* Would you input into your Google search keywords that would bring you back images and websites you find *un*pleasant, *dis*tasteful, or otherwise *un*wanted and *un*desirable to you? No.

The form of self-expression we seek is expressing *who we desire to be.*

If you are constantly angry, sad, bitter or jealous, then you are not "dialing up" in a manner that will elicit the response you want from life. Therefore, people who "can't help" but express themselves through negativity should not be shocked (although they usually are) when "bad things happen to them." But often they are confused when life answers them with harshness and difficulties. Control of your thoughts and emotions does not mean giving out fake smiles, phony anecdotes or shallow compliments.

Control of your thoughts and emotions means expressing only those thoughts and emotions that "dial in" the corresponding responses you want from life.

What if you wanted to dial your mother's phone number to hear a response of pleasantries, but you instead dial up your arch rival—*by mistake.* In that instant, you did not know how to use your machine (your iPhone) to get your desired results. *The problem is not in the phone.* You would not be silly enough to take the phone back to Apple and complain. No. The problem is in *you.*

There is something *you* did not get right—some misunderstanding on your part. And you didn't see how what *you did* while dialing in put you through to who you *didn't* want to respond. The unawareness of your ignorance is inconsequential, because the phone can only do what is asked of it, *even if the command is given by mistake or unintelligibly.* Maybe you stored the number wrong. Maybe you had the wrong area code. Maybe you didn't speak clearly into the voice dial. But it is your responsibility to figure it out, if you want the pleasant response.

Concerning the phone call, whatever the issue may be, you can likely easily figure it out, so that next time you get the response you want. But you must dial in properly.

Obviously, this example is an over-simplification of life. However it is oversimplified only because the machine that is the iPhone is overly simple when compared to the machine that is *you.* These principles of operating machinery are always the same. *You only get out the nature of what you put in. And if you never figure out how to use your machine to benefit you, the machine will only slow you down and stifle your expression, instead of provide convenience and self-expression.* Suffice to say, if you never figure out how to use the machine that is *you,* the best you can do is figure out how to deal with a long, hard struggle of a life—as best you can.

To be clear: You cannot *dial up* frustration, anger, bitterness, sadness, hopelessness, jealousy, fear, envy, and expect riches, good health, loving relationships, prosperous business, and so on, to *respond.* When you reactively dial-up that negative emotion out of anger or sheer frustration, and try to justify it by saying "I couldn't help it," or "that's just how I *feel,*" or "that's just what I *think,*" or "I'm just keeping it real," you certainly have every *right* to express yourself in that way.

This very right is the uniqueness of every human; the ability to choose independent thoughts and feelings. Free Will is the crown of the kingdom of man. But, keep in mind that whatever or whoever picks up on that other end is always going to be exactly who *you* called.

UNDERSTAND: Some people go through life experiencing continuous hardship and difficulty, not because they want those things, but because they are continuously "pocket-dialing" them.

Pocket Dialing

Pocket-dialing is when you *un*intentionally dial someone's number (usually by not paying attention while moving around or putting your phone in your pocket). When the person you unintentionally dialed picks up on the other end, and says, "Hello," you don't say anything because you didn't even know your phone was dialing the person. "Hello, hello, hello," he or she says. Finally, he hangs up, and may even call *you* back. This time, you hear the phone ringing, and you pick up. "*Hello?*," you say, as you are trying to figure out why this person is calling *you*. The person says, "*You just called me.*" And your response is, "*No I didn't,*" but then you look at your outgoing calls and sure enough, you *did* call that person, and so you say, "*Oh, I didn't call you on purpose. I must have pocket-dialed you. Sorry.*"

The point here is that when the circumstances of life "call our number," it doesn't make mistakes. Life knows our number and "calls us back" based on us calling it *first—whether we are **aware** of making the call it or not!* Whether or not this is "fair" is not the issue. As Bill Gates said, "*Life is not fair. Get used to it.*"

For those who experience continual failure, many fail to see their role in it, and deny they made the call in the first place. When something unwanted befalls—or "calls"—they feel victimized and "done wrong."

On the other hand, the successful man admits that he possibly made a mistake in "making the call," but then he also *takes responsibility for making the call* (because he understands the mechanism). Then he hangs up.

In every circumstance, no matter how "bad" it seems in the moment, *you* maintain the control of how you allow it to affect and stay with you. When you "clear the line" of the unintended bad, you "free up the line" for the *intentional* good. And because of this *responsibility* you take on, you now feel *empowered* to make the right calls in the future—knowing that life will surely call back. But we must get into the habit of knowing what we want and expressing (calling) those wants properly. If we do, the calls we receive will be from the things, people, and circumstances of our pleasure.

The purpose of the greatest machine ever—YOU—becomes more evident. You are here to express yourself—through yourself—**in the way you want**. The fundamental oversight is because you *are* the machine (say "I am")—you easily take *YOU* for granted.

As all other machines are *exterior* to us; it is so much easier to *see* the value and "smartness" in a $700 iPhone or the processing power in a $1,500 MacBook Pro, than to *see* the value and power in ourselves. Ironically, the blueprint and design of those machines that we so easily swoon over are attempting to copy the mechanism of *man.* Yet we so easily take ourselves for granted, for one simple reason: ***You cannot see your eye with your eye.*** Why? *You cannot* (without a mirror) *see the seer while it is doing the seeing.* We are blind to that which is so near that it simply *is us.*

I truly believe a purpose of living is to exude true expression of self in a manner that helps others express their truest self.

The beauty of this "human machine" is that if it is operated correctly—in a manner of true self-expression—everything else eventually takes care of itself. The material riches we seek begin to flow into our lives with ease. Material riches are necessary for self-expression. You will not find one without the other. No one wants to "work for a living." You are here to *live*, not to just "get by." And the purpose of money is to free up your time so that you are available to do what you enjoy doing.

When the human is operating as intended, the activity taking place is *self-expression* by the individual. Machines—in addition to performing an intended action—*produce something* in the process. This "something" can be either an intended product or simply a by-product—secondary in importance to the activity. And so it is for the human machine as well. If the human machine is operated properly, it will produce a product (or by-product) we commonly know as *time*.

People often say that wealth is expressed in time, not money. And the reason is simple: Having an abundance of money that will last for a very long time (aka wealth) *frees you up to do what you want to do with your time.* That's really what it boils down to. We are seeking *time*. If you are not expressing your true nature through self-expression, you do not truly have your *time*.

The concept of "time" is strictly man-made. But the reason may not be obviously clear. So we begin to see that time—as well as physical space (always a function of time)—is simply a by-product of the human mind. When did time begin? When will time end? How far does the vastness of the universe stretch? How small can we delve down past the extraordinarily minute structure of subatomic particles? These answers pertaining to time and space all have the same answer: *Infinity*. Infinitely big is the same as infinitely small. Infinitely long is the same is infinitely short. They are all undefined.

There is no "beginning" or "end" to time. There is no "end of the universe" or "small as small can get." There are no boundaries on either end. We have always kind of "known" this. We have always had to be somehow "okay" with not having any answers concerning the limits of space and time.

We can search and search and search, but only go crazy in pursuit of an answer, because an answer "does not exist." There "is no" limit on space and time. Huh? Why? The answer is simple. The boundaries of space and time do not exist simply because we cannot perceive the existence of those boundaries. And why can we not perceive those boundaries? We cannot perceive those boundaries because everything that we can perceive is perceived with our mind.

Ok. So why can't our mind perceive those boundaries—or origin? Because our mind IS the boundary! Our mind IS the origin.

Remember, as I am engaged in looking, I cannot see—or perceive—my eye with my eye. (I cannot see the one thing I use to do the seeing). For the same reason, as I am engaged in perceiving the boundary of space and time, I cannot perceive the boundary of space and time with my mind (I cannot perceive the one thing I use to do the perceiving). The mind is the boundary of space and time!

In other words, the mind cannot perceive the ultimate essence of the origin of all creation (which would be in terms of space and time), because the mind is the ultimate essence of the origin of all creation!

> It is not so much that space and time are *unlimited,*
> but that the human mind cannot *perceive* such
> a limit because the human mind *is* literally
> that limit. The human mind is literally
> *the beginning and end of all.*

Everywhere we *can* look, we *will* see something. As we daily look out into our world, our human perception of space and time is merely a reflection—a by-product—from the mechanism of our very own human mind. Things don't exist *outside* of the mind; they exist only as reflections caused by the Attractive Mechanism *of* the mind.

The mind itself is not something we can actually see, so our reflection looking out is the only clue to what our mind "looks like." This is just as sure as when we look out into the world, all that we see is a reflection from our eye—an eye that we cannot actually see. In both cases, only the reflections (caused by the mechanism) are seen, while the origin (the seer) remains unseen—*perfectly hidden by its unfathomable "nearness."* As James 4:8 reminds us, *Draw nigh unto God, and He will draw nigh unto you.*

A long time ago, a dear friend of mine would habitually gaze at me and ask, "Who *are* you?"

I was puzzled for years by this question. But now I have the answer. My answer is simply, "I am"—or more specifically, "*Eye* Am." I no longer feel *separate from God.*

About the Author

Kolie Crutcher is the founder and CEO of *GET MONEY Magazine* located on Wall Street in the heart of New York City's financial district. *GET MONEY* is the premier lifestyle magazine for the urban entrepreneur, and aims to guide the young adult onto the path of creating generational wealth.

Kolie is an alumnus of Mississippi State University, and has earned a Bachelor of Science Degree in electrical engineering, and mathematics. His in-depth understanding of electrical engineering principles and practical engineering experience forms the basis of his writings. His books and publications strive to verse the reader in the universal science and predictable mechanisms by which they can reliably become successful.

As an engineer, writer, publisher, and business owner in New York City, Kolie Crutcher is able to capture the attention of diverse people from all backgrounds, by speaking through the universal language of success.

He can be reached at www.koliecrutcher.com

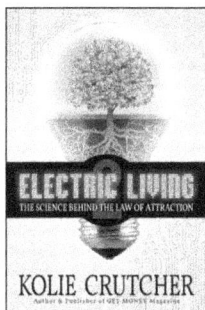

An electrical engineer by training, Crutcher applies his in-depth knowledge of electrical engineering principles and practical engineering experience detailing the scientific explanation of why human beings become what they think about. Addressing classic and quantum physics, the conscious and subconscious mind, infinite intelligence and free will, *Electric Living* deftly melds science and philosophy, giving readers a practical, step-by-step analysis for how to harness their thoughts and emotions so that the Law of Attraction will benefit them in their pursuit of success.

ISBN: 978-1-936332-58-8

Bettie Youngs Books

We specialize in MEMOIRS
. . . books that celebrate
fascinating people and
remarkable journeys

9 781940 784595